Christmas Gifts-in-a-Jar Cookbook

A Collection of Christmas Gifts-in-a-Jar Recipes

Gifts-in-a-Jar Cookbook Series – Book 1

Karen Jean Matsko Hood

Christmas Gifts-in-a-Jar Cookbook

A Collection of Christmas Gifts-in-a-Jar Recipes

Gifts-in-a-Jar Cookbook Series – Book 1

Karen Jean Matsko Hood

Published by

Whispering Pine Press International, Inc.
Your Northwest Book Publishing Company

2510 North Pines Road, Suite 206, Sales Room
Spokane Valley, WA 99206-7636 USA
Phone: (509) 928-7888 | Fax: (509) 922-9949
Email: sales@whisperingpinepress.com
Websites: www.WhisperingPinePress.com
www.WhisperingPinePressBookstore.com
Blog: www.WhisperingPinePressBlog.com
SAN 253-200X
Printed in the U.S.A.

Published by Whispering Pine Press International, Inc.
International Publishing Company
2510 North Pines Road, Suite 206, Sales Room
Spokane Valley, Washington 99206-7636 USA

For sales outside the United States, please contact the Whispering Pine Press International, Inc., International Sales Department.

Manufactured in the United States of America. This paper is acid-free and 100% chlorine free.

Book and Cover Design by Artistic Design Service, Inc.
Spokane Valley, WA 99206-7636 USA
www.ArtisticDesignService.com

Library of Congress Control Number (LCCN): 2014909196

Hood, Karen Jean Matsko
    Title: Christmas Gifts-in-a-Jar Cookbook, A Collection of Christmas Gifts-in-a-Jar Recipes, Gifts-in-a-Jar Cookbook Series – Book 1

ISBN: 978-1-59808-363-7   case bound
ISBN: 978-1-59808-364-4   perfect bound
ISBN: 978-1-59808-365-1   spiral bound
ISBN: 978-1-59808-367-5   E-PDF
ISBN: 978-1-59808-370-5   E-PUB
ISBN: 978-1-59808-371-2   E-PRC

First Edition: December 2014
1. Cookbook (*Christmas Gifts-in-a-Jar, A Collection of Christmas Gifts-in-a-Jar Recipes, Gifts-in-a-Jar Cookbook Series – Book 1*)

Christmas Gifts-in-a-Jar Cookbook
A Collection of Christmas Gifts-in-a-Jar Recipes
Gifts-in-a-Jar Cookbook Series – Book 1

Gift Inscription

To: _____

From: _____

Date: _____

Special Occasion: _____

Special Message:

_____

_____

_____

_____

_____

*It is always nice to receive a personal note to create a
special memory.*

www.WhisperingPinePress.com
www.WhisperingPinePressBookstore.com

Dedications

To my husband and best friend, Jim.

To our seventeen children: Gabriel, Brianne Kristina and her husband Moulik Vinodkumar Kothari, Marissa Kimberly and her husband Kevin Matthew Franck, Janelle Karina and her husband Paul Joseph Turcotte, Mikayla Karlene, Kyler James, Kelsey Katrina, Corbin Joel, Caleb Jerome, Keisha Kalani Hiwot, Devontay Joshua, Kianna Karielle Selam, Rosy Kiara, Mercedes Katherine, Jasmine Khalia Wengel, Cheyenne Krystal, and Annalise Kaylee Marie.

To Nola Paige, Zoey Karina, and future grandchildren.

To our foster grandchildren: Courtney, Lorenzo, and Leah.

To my brother, Stephen, and his wife, Karen.

To my husband's ten siblings: Gary, Colleen, John, Dan, Mary, Ray, Ann, Teresa, Barbara, Agnes, and their families.

In loving memory of my mom, who passed away in 2007; my dad, who passed away in 1976; and my sister, Sandy, who passed away due to multiple sclerosis in 1999.

To Sandy's three sons: Monte, Bradley, and Derek. To Monte's wife, Sarah, and their children: Liam, Alice, Charlie, and Samuel and their foster children. To Bradley's wife, Shawnda, and their children: Anton, Isaac, and Isabel.

To our foster children past and present: Krystal, Sara, Rebecca, Janice, Devontay Joshua, Mercedes Katherine, Zha'Nell, Makia, Onna, Cheyenne Krystal, Onna Marie, Nevaeh, and Zada, our future foster children, and all foster children everywhere.

To the Court Appointed Special Advocate (CASA) Volunteer Program in the judicial system which benefits abused and neglected children.

To the Literacy Campaign dedicated to promoting literacy throughout the world.

Christmas Gifts-in-a-Jar Cookbook

Table of Contents

Christmas Gifts-in-a-Jar Cookbook
A Collection of Christmas Gifts-in-a-Jar Recipes
Gifts-in-a-Jar Cookbook Series – Book 1

Introduction

Holidays are such an important time for families and friends. All holidays create special moments and memories to treasure. Homemade gifts are thoughtful ways to let the people in your life know you care about them during the holiday season. The uniqueness of home-made gifts inspired my Gifts-In-A-Jar Cookbook series.

The Gifts-in-a-Jar Cookbook Series would not be complete without *Christmas Gifts-in-a-Jar Cookbook,* because gifts-in-a-jar are popular and easy to make. They can also be made ahead and this can help avoid the last minute stress of shopping for gifts during the busy holiday season.

We hope you enjoy reading it as well as trying out all of the recipes. This cookbook is designed for easy use and is organized into alphabetical sections: appetizers and dips, beverages, breads and muffins, breakfast, cakes, candies, cookies, dressings, sauces, and condiments, jams, jellies, and syrups.

Do enjoy your holiday reading and recipe planning, but more importantly, have fun with those you care about while you are cooking and preparing gifts. Happy Holiday season from the author Karen Jean Matsko Hood.

Following is a collection of recipes gathered and modified by Karen Jean Matsko Hood.

Christmas Gifts-in-a-Jar Cookbook
A Collection of Christmas Gifts-in-a-Jar Recipes
Gifts-in-a-Jar Cookbook Series – Book 1

Poinsettia
Botanical Classification

Poinsettia Botanical Classification

Kingdom: *Plantae*
Division: *Magnoliophyta*
Class: *Magnoliopsida*
Order: *Malpighiales*
Family: *Euphorbiaceae*
Genus: *Euphorbia*
Species: *E. pulcherrima*
Binomial name: *Euphorbia pulcherrima*

Poinsettias are flowers found in the wild in deciduous tropical forests at moderate elevations from southern Sinaloa down the entire Pacific coast of Mexico to Chiapas and into Guatemala. It is also found in some parts of central southern Mexico in the hot, seasonally dry forests in Guerrero, Oaxaca, and a few localities in Guatemala.

They are named after Joel Roberts Poinsett, the first United States ambassador to Mexico, who introduced the plant in the United States in 1825. The Mexican poinsettia is known as the Christmas Flower in North America. The ancient Aztecs prized the poinsettia (cuetlaxochitl in Nahuatl) as a symbol of purity.

In Turkey, it is known as "Atatürk's Flower," since it is considered to be the favorite flower of Atatürk, the founder of modern Turkey.

Alternative names for the poinsettia are *Euphorbia pulcherrima*, Mexican Flame Leaf, Christmas Star, Winter Rose, Noche Buena, and Ataturk's Flower (in Turkey). In Nahuatl, one of the major languages spoken in central Mexico, the plant is called *Cuitlaxochitl*, meaning "excrement flower." The name may have come from the observation of birds that would eat the seeds, and then the flowers would appear to germinate from the bird excrement.

Cultivars have been produced with orange, pale green, cream, and marbled leaves.

Poinsettias are shrubs to small trees, typically reaching a height of 0.6 to 4 m (2 to 16 feet). The plant bears dark green dentate leaves that measure 7 to 16 cm (3 to 6 inches) in length. The top leaves, known as bracts, are flaming red, pink, or white and are often mistaken as flowers. The actual flowers are grouped within the small yellow structures found in the center of each leaf bunch, which are called *Cyathea*.

Christmas Gifts-in-a-Jar Cookbook
A Collection of Christmas Gift-in-a-Jar Recipes
Gifts-in-a-Jar Cookbook Series – Book 1

Caring for Your Poinsettia

Caring for Your Poinsettia

There are exactly 109 varieties of poinsettias available, but 69 percent of Americans still prefer red poinsettias, 7 percent prefer white, and 14 percent prefer pink.

A generally accepted standard is that the plant should be 2½ times taller than the diameter of the container.

Keep your poinsettias at a room temperature between 68 and 70 degrees F. Do not place your plant near cold drafts or excessive heat. Some places to avoid are near appliances, fireplaces, or ventilating ducts.

To protect your poinsettia from chilling winds when transporting plants, carry them in a large shopping bag.

Water thoroughly when the soil feels dry to the touch, but do not let plants sit in standing water. Over watering causes plants to droop.

To keep your plant after the holidays, fertilize after the blooming season with a balanced, all-purpose fertilizer. Do not fertilize when plants are in bloom.

Poinsettias need light, so place them in a bright place for at least six hours a day. In areas outside its natural environment, it is commonly grown as an indoor plant where it prefers good morning sun then shade in the hotter part of the day. However, it is widely grown and very popular in subtropical climates such as Sydney, Australia.

As this is a subtropical plant, it will likely perish if the nighttime temperature falls below 50 degrees F., so it is not suitable for planting in the ground in milder climates. Daytime temperatures in excess of 70 degrees F. tend to shorten the lifespan of the plant.

Your poinsettia can be difficult to induce to reflower after the initial display when purchased. The plant requires a period of uninterrupted long, dark nights for around two months in autumn in order to develop flowers. Incidental light at night during this time will hamper flower production.

Christmas Gifts-in-a-Jar Cookbook
A Collection of Christmas Gifts-in-a-Jar Recipes
Gifts-in-a-Jar Cookbook Series – Book 1

Christmas Facts

Christmas Facts

The Christmas Tree: The tradition of a holiday tree has been around since ancient times and has played an important part in winter celebrations for many centuries. Many pagan festivals used trees to honor gods and spirits. In Northern Europe the Vikings considered the evergreen a symbol and reminder that the darkness and cold of winter would end and the green of spring would return. The Druids of ancient England and France decorated oak trees with fruit and candles to honor their gods of harvests.

In 1841 the English royalty helped popularize the tree in England by decorating the first Christmas tree at Windsor Castle. Prince Albert, husband of Queen Victoria, decorated the first English Christmas Tree with candles, candies, fruits, and gingerbread.

We have taken the Christmas tree from Germany and gift giving from the Dutch tradition of leaving out wooden shoes for them to be filled with goodies. But one tradition remains universal: sharing and caring.

Christmas Colors: The colors most often associated with Christmas decorating are green, red, white, blue, silver, and gold. These colors have been used for centuries and, as with most traditions, the reason may be traced to religious beliefs. In this instance, green represents everlasting life, red represents the bloodline of Jesus Christ, blue represents the sky from which the angels appeared, white represents the purity of the Virgin Birth, and silver and gold represent the richness of God's Blessings.

Christmas Truce in the Midst of World War I: In 1914 there was a truce between German and British troops in France. Soldiers on both sides spontaneously began to sing Christmas carols and stopped fighting. The truce began on Christmas Day and continued for some time afterward. There was even a soccer game between the trench lines in which Germany's 133rd Royal Saxon Regiment is said to have beaten Britain's Seaforth Highlanders 3 to 2.

Christmas Gifts-in-a-Jar Cookbook

A Collection of Christmas Gifts-in-a-Jar Recipes
Gifts-in-a-Jar Cookbook Series – Book 1

Christmas Folklore

Christmas Folklore

Few Americans, to be sure, bother with a Yule log any longer; yet the Yule log was once one of the most firmly entrenched of customs. Often a stump or root, it was brought home Christmas Eve, where it was placed in the kitchen hearth or in the main fireplace. It was lighted with a faggot saved from the year before (lest the house burn down) and kept burning for twelve hours (lest ill luck come). It was not to be bought but was to be obtained from one's own land or from a neighbor's wood, and it had to ignite the first time (lest trouble follow). In some areas the "log" had to be ash, "the ashen faggot," usually a whole tree, cut up, bound, and drawn to the house by oxen. There it was burned, as people told ghost stories and tales of olden times.

There is another story about a war orphan living in an institution who wrote Santa Claus asking that "a real home" be found for him. The orphanage intercepted the letter, publicized it with comments such as "we've just got to find a home or deny the Santa Claus legend." Supposedly, over 100 families responded and were willing to take the child.

Other stories report dying children who have been visited by Santa Claus in September, October, or even June, because they would not live until late December.

More stories tell of hard-bitten soldiers playing Santa to captured enemy youngsters, and of homeless families who appealed to Santa to help them relocate. All testify to the power of our belief that people have an innate right to be visited by Santa Claus and that no effort to protect this right is too great to make. In fact, from 1914 to 1928, when it was investigated unfavorably by the postal authorities, a Santa Claus Association founded by John D. Gluck was not only able to flourish in New York City but was even copied in other towns. Its purpose was to get letters addressed to Santa Claus from the post offices, investigate the circumstances of the children involved, and do for the youngsters whatever was expected.

Christmas Gifts-in-a-Jar Cookbook
A Collection of Christmas Gifts-in-a-Jar Recipes
Gifts-in-a-Jar Cookbook Series – Book 1

Christmas History

Christmas History

The story of Christmas begins with the birth of a baby in Bethlehem. It is believed that Christ was born on the 25th, although the exact month is unknown. It was in 350 A.D. that December 25 was declared the official date for celebrating Christmas by Pope Julius I.

Members of the pagan order have always celebrated the Winter Solstice, the season of the year when days are shortest and nights longest. It was generally believed to be a time of drunkenness, revelry, and debauchery. The pagan Romans called this celebration Saturnalia, in honor of their god Saturn. The festivities began in the middle of December and continued until January 1st. On December 25th, "The Birth of the Unconquerable Sun" was celebrated, as the days gradually lengthened and the sun began to regain its dominance. It is a general pagan belief that the sun dies during the Winter Solstice and then rises from the dead. With cries of "Jo Saturnalia!" the Roman celebration would include masquerades in the streets, magnificent festive banquets, the visiting of friends and the exchange of good-luck gifts known as *Strenae* (lucky fruits). Roman halls would be decked with garlands of laurel and green trees and adorned with lighted candles. Again, as with *Sacaea*, the masters and slaves would exchange places.

Saturnalia was considered a fun and festive time for the Romans, but Christians believed it an abomination to honor such a pagan god. The early converts wanted to maintain the birthday of their Christ Child as a solemn and religious holiday...not one of cheer and merriment, as was the pagan celebration of Saturnalia.

As Christianity spread, however, the church became alarmed by the continuing practice among its flock to indulge in pagan customs and celebrate the festival of Saturnalia. At first, the holy men prohibited this type of revelry, but it was to no avail. Eventually, a decision was made to tame such celebrations and make them into a festive occasion better suited to honor Christ.

Christmas Gifts-in-a-Jar Cookbook
A Collection of Christmas Gifts-in-a-Jar Recipes
Gifts-in-a-Jar Cookbook Series – Book 1

Christmas Symbols

Christmas Symbols

Fir Tree: The pure green color of the stately fir tree remains green all year round, depicting the everlasting hope of mankind. All the needles point toward heaven, making it a symbol of man's thoughts turning toward heaven.

The Star: The star was the heavenly sign of promises long ago. God promised a Savior for the world, and the star was the sign of fulfillment of His promise.

Candle: The candle symbolizes that Christ is the light of the world, and when we see this great light we are reminded of He who displaces the darkness.

Wreath: The wreath symbolizes the real nature of love. Real love never ceases. Love is one continuous round of affection.

Santa Claus: Santa Claus symbolizes the generosity and good will we feel during the month of December.

Holly Leaf: The holly plant represents immortality and the crown of thorns worn by our Savior. The red holly berries represent the bloodshed by Him.

The Gift: God so loved the world that He gave His only begotten Son. Thanks be to God for his unspeakable gift.

Wise Men: The wise men bowed before the Holy Babe and presented Him with gold, frankincense, and myrrh. We should always give gifts in the same spirit of the wise men.

Candy Cane: The candy cane represents the shepherds' crook. The crook on the staff helps to bring back strayed sheep to the flock. The candy cane is the symbol that we are our brother's keeper.

Angels: The angels heralded the glorious news of the Savior's birth. The angels sang glory to God in the highest, on earth peace and good will toward men.

Bell: The lost sheep are found by the sound of the bell; it should ring mankind to the fold. The bell symbolizes guidance and return.

Christmas Gifts-in-a-Jar Cookbook

A Collection of Christmas Gifts-in-a-Jar Recipes
Gifts-in-a-Jar Cookbook Series – Book 1

Christmas around the World

Christmas around the World

Germany: Many Christmas practices originate in Germanic countries, including the Christmas tree, the Christmas ham, the Yule log, holly, mistletoe, and the giving of presents.

Australia's Bondi Beach: In the southern hemisphere, Christmas is during the summer. This clashes with the traditional winter iconography, resulting in oddities such as a red fur-coated Santa Claus surfing in for a turkey barbecue.

Japan has adopted Santa Claus for its secular Christmas celebration, but New Year's Day is a far more important holiday.

In India, Christmas is often called bada din ("the big day"), and celebration revolves around Santa Claus and shopping.

In South Korea, Christmas is celebrated as an official holiday.

In The Netherlands, Germany, Scandinavia, Poland, and Lithuania, Christmas Day and the following day are called First and Second Christmas Day.

In Finland, Ireland, Italy, Romania, Austria, and Catalonia (Spain), the day after Christmas is known as St. Stephen's Day.

In Australia, Britain, New Zealand, and Canada December 26th is a holiday. Boxing Day began in England, in the middle of the nineteenth century, under Queen Victoria. Also known as St. Stephen's Day, it was a way for the upper class to give gifts of cash, or other goods, to those of the lower classes.

Several Latin American countries (such as Venezuela) believe that while Santa makes the toys, he then gives them to the Baby Jesus, who is the one who actually delivers them to the children's homes.

In many countries, children leave empty containers for Santa to fill with small gifts such as toys, candy, or fruit.

Children in some countries put their empty shoes out for Santa to fill on the night before Christmas.

Christmas Gifts-in-a-Jar Cookbook
A Collection of Christmas Gifts-in-a-Jar Recipes
Gifts-in-a-Jar Cookbook Series – Book 1

Poetry

A Collection of Poetry with Christmas Themes

Table of Contents

Page

Merry Christmas!

The air is cool, the season is snow.
Soon Christmas will come to us who know.
The elves are running for things to do.
In fact, these elves brought this to you!

"Merry Christmas" is a treasure from the Christmas hour
Just leave it up and watch its power.
In your house is where it works,
It cheers up those who stand and lurk.

These yummy treats are for your pleasure,
We've even included a little treasure.
Make two copies to give your friends
They'll have warm fuzzies that never end.

We'll all have a smile upon our face
No one will know who "Merry Christmas'd" this place.
Just one short day, your spell to cast
Or a big snowball will strike you fast!

And don't forget a nifty treat
Like something cute or something sweet.
Please join the fun, let's really hear it.
And spread some Merry Christmas and Christmas Spirit!

Directions:
- Enjoy treats!
- Leave the "Merry Christmas" on your front door.
- Now you have 24 hours to copy this twice, make the Christmas signs and two treat bags…
- Deliver them to two neighbors who don't have a "Merry Christmas" sign.
- Watch how far it goes!

Karen Jean Matsko Hood ©2014
Published in *Christmas Gifts-in-a-Jar Cookbook*, 2014
By Whispering Pine Press International, Inc., 2014

Christmas Eve

Twinkle of night stars
      bring hope

To souls each day
      in prayer.

Spirits rest under morning noon
      in darkness

Peace of night brings gentle breeze,
      in praise

As the sun rises and
      calls all to stand

             Rejoice
                in Christmas light.

Karen Jean Matsko Hood ©2014
Published in *Christmas Gifts-in-a-Jar Cookbook*, 2014
By Whispering Pine Press International, Inc., 2014

Golden Bows

Maple leaves twirl
Circling tendrils on a stem
Suddenly drop and lay still.

Golden bows on boxes
Foil wraps stars that twinkle
Christmas will soon be here.

Will we mail the cards
And wrap the gifts
Place the presents safe?

Remember it is the season
To remember the reason
And why golden bows exist.

Karen Jean Matsko Hood ©2014
Published in *Christmas Gifts-in-a-Jar Cookbook*, 2014
By Whispering Pine Press International, Inc., 2014

Christmas Cactus

Bright pink blossoms unfurl
Painted with fluted edges,
Enthusiastically open to sing
Beautiful melodies bold.
Vivid fuchsia blooms and flames
As they hang in ones and twos,
Artistic advent silhouettes
Against craggy, scalloped frames.

Christmas cactus stems,
Succulent and old,
Shrivel in spots like granny's face
Yet shout the youth of green.

Blossoms of antique lace distend
With morning sunshine.
Birth of the season, chortling delight,
Friendly with tenderness.

Christmas cactus foliage
Lines my way,
Liver-spotted, yet
Bright and young.

Karen Jean Matsko Hood ©2014
Published in *Christmas Gifts-in-a-Jar Cookbook*, 2014
By Whispering Pine Press International, Inc., 2014

Christmas Sweets

Sugar crystals sparkle on an antique silver spoon.
Mom selects brown sugar, white sugar,
confectioner's sugar, crystals, and more.
Granules sparkle white as snow.
Sugar with sweetness that entices your tongue.
Decorations garnish plum fairies,
that dance in your head.
Sugar coats the bristles of paint brushes
as the hand embellishes the palette of old.
Color enlivens his canvas with this
glint of sweetness as he wipes away
his tears of pain. Christmas toys lay
blanketed in white as elves
scurry under the tree.
Visions of fairies that
tiptoe on gossamer wings,
memories of kings
that run by queens.
Christmas dreams.

Karen Jean Matsko Hood ©2014
Published in *Christmas Gifts-in-a-Jar Cookbook*, 2014
By Whispering Pine Press International, Inc., 2014

Shipping Season Continues

Packages ship throughout the year:
Small ones, big ones, short ones, fat ones.
Don't forget the red seal;
bind them up with fiberglass tape.
They cannot break.

Foster child Susie goes to 42nd street;
bundle her up and send her ground.
Air expenses would cost the state
far too much, so "ground" she goes.

Pick up foster child Johnny
from 32nd and drop him in the large box.
Billy goes to 53rd via parcel post;
don't forget the bubble wrap.

Across the conveyor belt he goes,
carefully down the chute.
Oh, a call for a group of siblings
arrives. Can they ship all three?

No box on hand stands tall enough
To pack the trio today.
The state says we must ship right now,
so separate the three we must.

Sibling O, we'll put in box size R;
sibling P we'll stuff in box size H,
sibling A just barely fits in box N.
Hurry, we must get them on their way.

Out the door they go.
Shipping master worries:
What if they get damaged?
Who will pay the price?

Karen Jean Matsko Hood ©2014
Published in *Christmas Gifts-in-a-Jar Cookbook*, 2014
By Whispering Pine Press International, Inc., 2014

Candle Flicker

Sweet beeswax of Christmas candles trickle,
as the fluid flame polishes still.

Darkness smothers the flicker;
it can curl no more.

Dreams of life spiral from the
sleepiness of mind,

In wait of the Christmas star
specks of dust escape all time,

Water condenses on the windowpane,
and seeps down to warp the sill.

Mildew in the tiniest crevices
punctuates the air with the smell of discord.

Ink pen in hand and blank paper,
mellow tacit evening moments.

Christmas glow
and thoughtful memories.

Karen Jean Matsko Hood ©2014
Published in *Christmas Gifts-in-a-Jar Cookbook*, 2014
By Whispering Pine Press International, Inc., 2014

God Sent Children

Gifts in bundles that run on little legs
with mismatched socks and scraped knees;

Packages of chubby voices
bundled in throats that scream with glee;

Some with pigtails and freckled noses,
others in crew cuts and fair skin.

Brilliant as the crimson cardinal on a snowy branch,
Loving as the caress of wind on a winter day.

Thank you for the gifts
in jolly packages with calico faces.

Christmas gifts of children
Winter love.

Karen Jean Matsko Hood ©2014
Published in *Christmas Gifts-in-a-Jar Cookbook*, 2014
By Whispering Pine Press International, Inc., 2014

Christmas Walk Within

Do we really live in the spirit
Ever, sometimes, never?

Or do we only live
in the flesh

Always, usually, often?
How can we live better

in faith and love
to nourish

our souls?
When can we develop

a sense of reality
While a spirit walks

On clouds instead of
within our hearts?

Can we call for
the return of grace?

This Christmas
…or do we have to wait?

Karen Jean Matsko Hood ©2014
Published in *Christmas Gifts-in-a-Jar Cookbook*, 2014
By Whispering Pine Press International, Inc., 2014

Christmas Gifts-in-a-Jar Cookbook
A Collection of Christmas Gifts-in-a-Jar Recipes
Gifts-in-a-Jar Cookbook Series – Book 1

Christmas Traditions

Christmas Traditions

Early Christmas trees were often decorated with apples, nuts, cookies, colored popcorn, and candles. The invention of electricity in the early twentieth century and use of electrical Christmas lights helped spread the use of the Christmas tree.

Boxing Day: In English-speaking countries, the day following Christmas Day is called "Boxing Day." This word comes from the custom which started in the Middle Ages around 800 years ago: churches would open their "alms boxe" (boxes in which people had placed gifts of money) and distribute the contents to poor people in the neighborhood on the day after Christmas. The tradition continues today - small gifts are often given to delivery workers such as postal staff and children who deliver newspapers.

The legend of Santa Claus was brought by Dutch settlers to New York in the early eighteenth century. Santa Claus was depicted as a tall, dignified, religious figure riding a white horse through the air. Known as Saint Nicholas in Germany, he was usually accompanied by Black Peter, an elf who punished disobedient children. In North America he eventually developed into a fat, jolly old gentleman who had neither the religious attributes of Saint Nicholas nor the strict disciplinarian character of Black Peter.

Christmas cards: The custom of sending Christmas cards started in Britain in 1840 when the first "Penny Post" public postal deliveries began. As printing methods improved, Christmas cards were produced in large numbers from about 1860. They became even more popular in Britain when a card could be posted in an unsealed envelope for one half-penny - half the price of an ordinary letter.

Stamps are distributed each year by many nations to commemorate Christmas.

Christmas Gifts-in-a-Jar Cookbook
A Collection of Christmas Gifts-in-a-Jar Recipes
Gifts-in-a-Jar Cookbook Series – Book 1

Appetizers and Dips

Table of Contents

Bar Nuts Mix-in-a-Jar

This nut mix is great right out of the jar, or it can be warmed in the oven before serving. You may substitute an equal amount of unsalted assorted nuts for those listed in this recipe.

Ingredients:

1¾	lb. unsalted nuts, assorted
¼	lb. peanuts, peeled
¼	lb. cashews
¼	lb. brazil nuts
¼	lb. walnuts
¼	lb. hazelnuts
¼	lb. pecans
¼	lb. whole almonds, unpeeled
2	Tbs. fresh rosemary, coarsely chopped
½	tsp. cayenne
2	tsp. dark brown sugar
2	tsp. salt or to taste
1	Tbs. butter, melted

Directions:

1. Preheat oven to 350 degrees F.
2. In large bowl, toss nuts to combine; spread out on baking sheet.
3. Bake 15 to 18 minutes until light golden brown.
4. In large bowl, combine rosemary, cayenne, brown sugar, salt, and melted butter.
5. Thoroughly toss warm toasted nuts with spiced butter.

Yields: 5 cups.

Directions for Tag

1. For warm Bar Nuts, spread jar contents onto baking sheet and place in 300 degrees F. oven for 5 minutes.
2. These Bar Nuts are delicious right out of the jar. Just empty into serving bowl and enjoy!

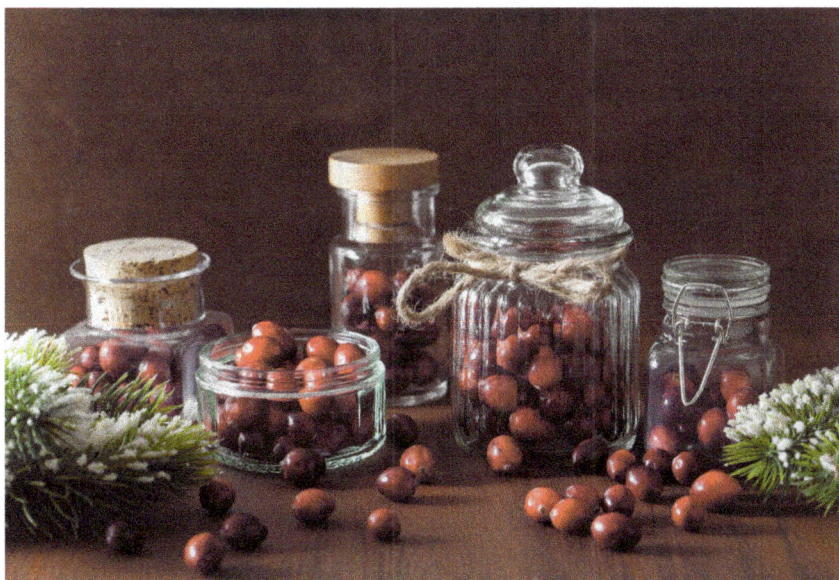

Beer Pretzels Mix-in-a-Jar

Pretzels are a festive low-fat treat for any occasion. Enjoy!

Ingredients:

3⅓	c. all-purpose flour
2	tsp. granulated sugar
1	pkg. yeast
1	tsp. salt
1	tsp. basil
¼	tsp. garlic powder
1	Tbs. dried onion
¾	c. parmesan cheese

Directions:

1. In large bowl, combine flour, sugar, yeast, and salt.
2. In small bowl, stir together basil, garlic, onion, and cheese.
3. Divide ingredients equally among 2 16-ounce jars.

Yields: 2 gifts.

Directions for Tag

Ingredients:

1	jar Beer Pretzels Mix
6	oz. beer (¾ c.)

Directions:

1. Preheat oven to 400 degrees.
2. Empty jar contents into mixing bowl.
3. Stir together the beer and jar mix.
4. Knead on lightly floured surface until smooth.
5. Cover and let rest in a warm area until doubled, about 45 minutes.

6. Roll dough out on lightly floured surface into a 10 x 6-inch rectangle; cut lengthwise into 6 strips.
7. Shape each strip into pretzel shape.
8. Cover and let rise again until nearly doubled, about 30 minutes.
9. Bake on top rack oven 8 minutes until lightly golden.
10. Transfer to wire rack to cool.

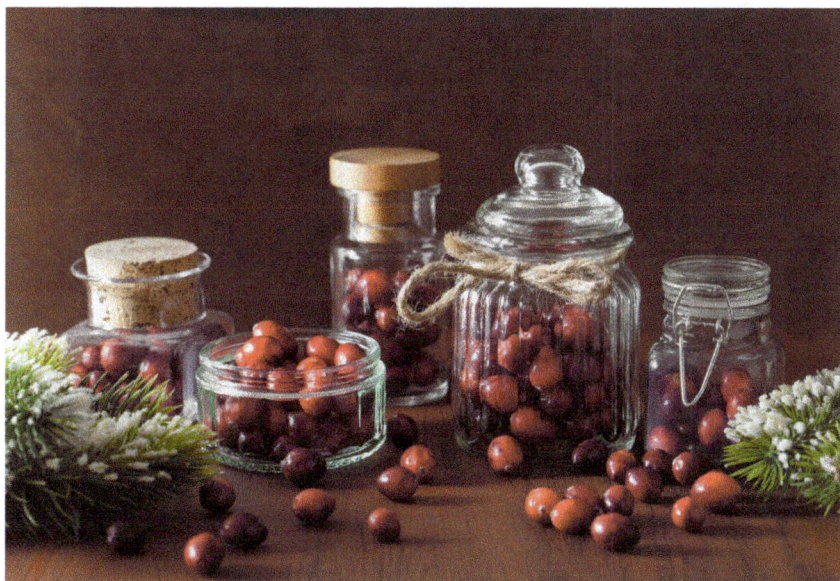

Butter Crackers Mix-in-a-Jar

Homemade crackers are a unique treat. This simple gift-in-a-jar will be enjoyed by the lucky person that receives it.

Ingredients:

3	c. flour
¾	c. butter
3	Tbs. sugar
1	tsp. salt
1	c. milk

Directions:

1. Preheat oven to 300 degrees F.
2. In large bowl, crumble first 4 ingredients together with your fingers. Add enough milk to make stiff dough.
3. Roll out dough as thin as possible and cut crackers with a cookie cutter.
4. Line a baking sheet with baking parchment and set the crackers on it. Can be placed close together as they do not spread.
5. If you want flat crackers, prick tops with a fork.
6. If you prefer to have them bubble slightly, leave them alone.
7. Bake 6 to 8 minutes until golden. Allow crackers to cool completely before putting into a jar, or they will turn soggy.

Directions for Tag

1. Transfer crackers to serving plate and enjoy. Or, eat them right out of the jar!

Caramel Peanut Butter Dip Mix-in-a-Jar

This recipe is easy to make and fun. Children especially love this combination.

Ingredients:

30	caramels
3	c. plus 2 Tbs. creamy peanut butter
3	c. peanuts, finely crushed

Directions:

1. Unwrap caramels and place in jar.
2. Add creamy peanut butter and finely crushed peanuts.

Directions for Tag

Ingredients:

1	jar Caramel Peanut Butter Dip Mix
1-2	Tbs. water
	sliced apples

Directions:

1. Empty jar mix into microwave-safe bowl.
2. Add water and microwave on high for 1 minute.
3. Stir. Microwave 1 to 2 minutes more and stir until smooth.
4. Serve warm with apples.

Yields: 1 cup.

Cheddar Cheese Twists Mix-in-a-Jar

Children of all ages seem to enjoy cheese snacks. This is a unique gift to give.

Ingredients:

1	c. sifted flour
1½	tsp. baking powder
½	tsp. salt
	dash ground cayenne pepper

Directions:

1. In medium bowl, sift flour, baking powder, salt, and cayenne pepper.
2. Pour into jar.

Directions for Tag

Ingredients:

1	jar Cheddar Cheese Twists Mix
2	Tbs. butter
½	c. sharp Cheddar cheese, shredded
⅓	c. cold water

Directions:

1. Preheat oven to 425 degrees F.
2. In large bowl, pour Cheddar Cheese Twists Mix.
3. Cut in butter and cheese with pastry cutter until mixture is crumbly.
4. Sprinkle cold water over mixture; mix lightly with fork until mixture holds together and leaves side of bowl.
5. Roll out to a rectangle 12 x 10-inches on a lightly floured board.

6.   Divide in half lengthwise, cut crosswise into strips ½-inch wide.
7.   Lift strips carefully and twist gently. Place twists 1 inch apart on ungreased baking sheets.
8.   Bake 10 minutes to light brown.
9.   Carefully transfer twists to wire racks to cool.

Cherry Orange Snack Mix-in-a-Jar

You can substitute dried cranberries, raisins, or currants for the dried cherries in this delicious snack mix.

Ingredients:

2	c. rice cereal squares
1	can salted mixed nuts (12 oz.)
2	egg whites
2	Tbs. orange juice
1¼	c. sugar
1	tsp. cinnamon
¼	c. butter
1½	c. dried cherries

Directions:

1. Preheat oven to 275 degrees F.
2. In large bowl, combine cereal and mixed nuts.
3. In medium bowl, beat egg whites, orange juice, sugar, and cinnamon until very soft peaks form.
4. Pour over cereal mixture and stir to mix well.
5. Melt butter in 15 x 10-inch jellyroll pan.
6. Spread cereal mixture in prepared pan.
7. Bake 30 minutes, stirring twice during baking.
8. Stir in dried cherries and bake 10 to 15 minutes longer until mixture is lightly browned and crisp.
9. Cool completely, break up into small chunks.
10. Put this delicious chewy, crunchy, and sweet snack mix into a decorative jar for a wonderful gift.

Directions for Tag

1. Transfer snack mix to serving bowl and enjoy. Or, eat it right out of the jar!

Christmas Pecans Mix-in-a-Jar

These flavored pecans will be appreciated by the receiver. Make sure they are cool and dry before packing in a canning jar and labeling for a favorite gift.

Ingredients:

1	egg white
2	c. pecan halves
½	c. light brown sugar, firmly packed
2	tsp. grated orange rind
2	Tbs. fresh orange juice
½	tsp. salt
¼	tsp. cinnamon
	cooking spray

Directions:

1. Preheat oven to 325 degrees F.
2. In medium bowl, whisk egg white until frothy; toss with pecans and drain well.
3. In large bowl, stir together brown sugar and next four ingredients. Add pecans and toss.
4. Place pecans in a single layer on an aluminum foil-lined baking sheet coated with cooking spray.
5. Bake 30 minutes, stirring occasionally.
6. Cool completely and place in canning jar.

Yields: 2 cups.

Directions for Tag

1. Transfer pecans to serving bowl and enjoy. Or, eat them right out of the jar!

Cranberry Raisin Snack Mix-in-a-Jar

This snack mix makes a colorful, crunchy gift. Make sure you cool and dry it completely before packing it in your gift jars.

Ingredients:

½	c. butter
⅓	c. honey
¼	c. brown sugar, packed
1	tsp. ground cinnamon
½	tsp. salt
3	c. square oat cereal
1½	c. old-fashioned oats
1	c. walnuts, chopped
½	c. dried cranberries
½	c. chocolate-covered raisins

Directions:

1. Preheat oven to 275 degrees F.
2. In saucepan or microwave-safe bowl, combine first 5 ingredients; heat until butter is melted.
3. Stir until sugar is dissolved.
4. In large bowl, combine cereal, oats, and nuts.
5. Drizzle with butter mixture and mix well.
6. Place in a greased 15 x 10-inch baking pan.
7. Bake uncovered 45 minutes, stirring every 15 minutes.
8. Cool 15 minutes, stirring occasionally.
9. Stir in cranberries and chocolate-covered raisins.
10. Cool completely and divide into 3 gift jars.

Yields: 6 cups.

Directions for Tag

1. Transfer snack mix to serving bowl and enjoy. Or, eat it right out of the jar!

Dill Dip Mix-in-a-Jar

This dip is easy-to-make and is delicious. Simply use the best ingredients you can find, and put them in a decorative jar of your choice. This dip is excellent for chips or fresh veggies. It also makes a great topping for baked potatoes.

Ingredients:

- ½ c. dried dill weed
- ½ c. dried minced onion
- ½ c. dried parsley
- ⅓ c. Beau Monde seasoning

Directions:

1. Combine all ingredients and pour into a jar.

Directions for Tag

Ingredients:

- 3 Tbs. Dill Dip Mix
- 1 c. mayonnaise
- 1 c. sour cream

Directions:

1. In medium bowl, using wire whisk, combine dill dip mix, mayonnaise, and sour cream.
2. Refrigerate dip until ready to serve.
3. Serve with chips or fresh veggies, or as a topping for baked potatoes.

Honey Roasted Holiday Mix-in-a-Jar

This holiday mix of peanuts, chow mein noodles, and popcorn will be enjoyed and appreciated by the recipient.

Ingredients:

6	c. popcorn
1	can wide chow mein noodles (5 oz.)
5	Tbs. butter
3	Tbs. granulated sugar
1	tsp. vanilla extract
½	tsp. cinnamon
1	c. peanuts, honey roasted

Directions:

1. Preheat oven to 250 degrees F.
2. In large roasting pan, mix popcorn and chow mein noodles.
3. In small saucepan, melt butter and sugar together; stir in vanilla and cinnamon.
4. Pour over popcorn, toss to coat.
5. Bake 1 hour, stirring every 20 minutes.
6. Add nuts. Spread on paper towels to cool.
7. Place into gift jars after completely cooled.

Yields: 11 cups.

Directions for Tag

1. Transfer snack mix to serving bowl and enjoy. Or, eat it right out of the jar!

Hot and Spicy Chex Party Mix-in-a-Jar

My children always love chex mixes and this makes an affordable gift-in-a-jar that is easy to make.

Ingredients:

¼	c. butter
1	Tbs. Worcestershire sauce
2-3	tsp. Tabasco Pepper Sauce
1¼	tsp. seasoned salt
2⅔	c. corn chex cereal
2⅔	c. rice chex cereal
2⅔	c. wheat chex cereal
1	c. mixed nuts
1	c. pretzels
1	c. cheese crackers, bite-size

Directions:

1. Preheat oven to 250 degrees F.
2. In open roasting pan in oven, melt butter; stir in seasonings.
3. Gradually add cereals, nuts, pretzels, and cheese crackers; stir to coat evenly.
4. Bake 1 hour, stirring every 15 minutes.
5. Spread on absorbent paper to cool.
6. Place into gift jars.

Yields: 11 cups.

Directions for Tag

1. Transfer snack mix to serving bowl and enjoy. Or, eat it right out of the jar!

Onion Dip Mix-in-a-Jar

Onion dip is a Hood family favorite and this makes a nice mix to have on hand.

Ingredients:

6	onion bouillon cubes, crushed
2	beef bouillon cubes, crushed
4	tsp. cornstarch
⅔	c. instant onion flakes
4	dashes pepper

Directions:

1. Mix together all ingredients and place in a jar.

Yields: 2 batches.

Directions for Tag

Ingredients:

½	jar Onion Dip Mix
2	c. sour cream

Directions:

1. Mix onion mix with sour cream.
2. Chill before serving.
3. Can be served with any type of snacks for dipping: crackers, pretzels, breadsticks, chips, and your favorite fresh vegetables.

Orient Express Mix-in-a-Jar

This recipe has some Asian flavor for a quick snack mix.

Ingredients:

3	Tbs. butter
1	Tbs. peanut butter
2	Tbs. soy sauce
1	tsp. brown sugar, packed
½	tsp. garlic powder
½	tsp. dry mustard
½	tsp. ground ginger
5	c. bite-size corn or rice cereal or a combination
1	c. chow mein noodles
1-2	Tbs. sliced almonds, optional

Directions:

1. In large microwave-safe bowl, melt butter and peanut butter on high.
2. Stir in soy sauce, sugar, garlic, mustard, and ginger.
3. Gradually add cereal, noodles, and almonds; stir until all pieces are evenly coated.
4. Microwave on high 3½ to 4 minutes, stirring thoroughly every minute scraping sides and bottom of bowl.
5. Spread on absorbent paper to cool.
6. Divide cooled mix into 2 jars.

Directions for Tag

1. Transfer snack mix to serving bowl and enjoy. Or, eat it right out of the jar!

Party Nibbles Mix-in-a-Jar

This mix is very easy-to-make. Once again, make sure it is thoroughly cool and dry before packing into jars. All your gift recipients have to do is simply open and enjoy.

Ingredients:

1	pkg. seasoned croutons (6 oz.)
1	pkg. fish-shaped crackers (6 oz.)
1	pkg. pretzel twists (6½ oz.)
1	can mixed nuts (12 oz.)
¾	c. butter, melted
1	tsp. hickory flavored salt
¼	tsp. garlic powder

Directions:

1. Preheat oven to 250 degrees F.
2. In large roasting pan, combine first 4 ingredients; stir well.
3. Combine last 3 ingredients; stir well. Drizzle over nut mixture; stir well.
4. Bake 1 hour, stirring every 15 minutes.
5. Cool completely, place into jars.

Yields: 3 quarts.

Directions for Tag

1. Transfer snack mix to serving bowl and enjoy. Or, eat it right out of the jar!

Raging Cajun Party Mix-in-a-Jar

This simple snack mix is inexpensive to make and will be a welcomed gift to anyone.

Ingredients:

1	tsp. chili powder
½	tsp. onion powder
½	tsp. garlic powder
¼	tsp. salt
⅛	tsp. cayenne pepper
1	bag (3-3½ oz.) microwave popcorn, popped (8-9 c.)
2	c. mini pretzels
2	c. toasted corn cereal squares

Directions:

1. In small cup, combine chili, onion and garlic powders, salt, and cayenne pepper.
2. Discard unpopped kernels, and sprinkle seasonings over popcorn; mix to coat evenly.
3. In large bowl, toss coated popcorn, pretzels, and cereal until well mixed.
4. Place into gift jars and decorate!

Directions for Tag

1. Transfer snack mix to serving bowl and enjoy. Or, eat it right out of the jar!

Roasted Almonds Mix-in-a-Jar

Many people like the taste of roasted almonds, and these are very simple to make.

Ingredients:

2	Tbs. liquid smoke, to taste
3	lb. raw almonds
2	Tbs. canola oil
	seasoning salt, to taste
	sea salt, to taste

Directions:

1. Preheat oven to 250 degrees F.
2. Place 2 tablespoons liquid smoke on large baking sheet.
3. Stir in ½ bag of almonds; spread out on sheet.
4. Stir in 2 tablespoons canola oil; spread out on sheet.
5. Season to taste, spread out on baking sheet.
6. Roast 1½ hour.
7. Remove from oven and spread single layer on newspaper to soak up oil.
8. When completely cool, place in 1-quart bag or jar.

Directions for Tag

1. Transfer snack mix to serving bowl and enjoy. Or, eat it right out of the jar!

Sesame Cheese Dip Mix-in-a-Jar

This dip has great flavor with the addition of toasted sesame seeds and celery seed for a unique gift dip.

Ingredients:

2	Tbs. parmesan cheese, grated
4	tsp. toasted sesame seeds
1	tsp. salt
1	tsp. celery seed
2	dash pepper
¼	tsp. garlic powder

Directions:

1. Measure all ingredients into a jar.
2. Shake well to blend seasoning.

Directions for Tag

Ingredients:

2	Tbs. Sesame Cheese Dip Mix
1	c. sour cream

Directions:

1. In small bowl, combine Sesame Cheese Dip Mix with sour cream.
2. Chill at least 1 hour before serving with snack crackers and fresh vegetables.

Yields: 2 batches.

Spiced Nuts Mix-in-a-Jar

Use your favorite type of nut to make this spicy holiday treat.

Ingredients:

5	c. nuts of your choice
¼	c. canola oil
1	Tbs. cumin
¼	tsp. cayenne pepper
¼	c. sugar
2	tsp. salt

Directions:

1. Preheat oven to 300 degrees F.
2. Place nuts in a bowl.
3. In small heavy saucepan, add oil; place over medium-low heat until warm.
4. Add cumin and cayenne; stir until mixture is aromatic, about 15 seconds.
5. Pour flavored oil over nuts.
6. Add sugar and salt; stir to coat evenly.
7. Transfer nuts to large baking sheet.
8. Bake, stirring occasionally until nuts are toasted, about 20 minutes.
9. Pour cooled nuts into wide-mouth canning jars for up to 2 weeks room temperature, or 2 months in freezer.

Directions for Tag

1. Nuts may be poured into a serving dish right out of the jar, or they may be warmed 5 minutes in a 300 degrees F. oven.

Spicy Crunch Mix-in-a-Jar

This version of chex mix uses pretzel nuggets and peanuts for variety. The cayenne, chili powder, and curry add extra flavor and spice.

Ingredients:

2	c. crunchy wheat chex cereal
2	c. crunchy corn chex cereal
2	c. pretzel nuggets
1	c. peanuts
6	Tbs. butter
1	tsp. cayenne
1	tsp. chili powder
1	tsp. curry
	salt, to taste

Directions:

1. Preheat oven to 350 degrees F.
2. In large bowl, mix cereals, pretzels, and nuts.
3. In small saucepan, melt butter and add seasonings.
4. Drizzle butter mixture over cereal mixture and toss to coat; season with salt.
5. Bake 20 minutes; remove and cool completely.
6. Place cooled mix into gift jars.

Yield: 7 cups

Directions for Tag

1. Transfer snack mix to serving bowl and enjoy. Or, eat it right out of the jar!

Sweet-n-Spicy Nuts Mix-in-a-Jar

This version blends the savory flair of cayenne in contrast with the sweetness of brown sugar to flavor your favorite mix of nuts.

Ingredients:

2	c. mixed nuts, unsalted
1½	Tbs. butter
2	Tbs. brown sugar, firmly packed
1½	Tbs. granulated sugar
½	tsp. cayenne
½	tsp. pepper, freshly ground
1	tsp. salt

Directions:

1. In heavy skillet, cook nuts in butter over moderate heat, stirring 2 minutes.
2. In small bowl, stir together sugars, cayenne, black pepper, and salt; sprinkle mixture over nuts.
3. Continue to cook nuts, stirring constantly, until sugar caramelizes, about 8 minutes.
4. Transfer nuts to sheet of foil and cool.
5. Break nuts apart and place into jar.

Yields: 2 cups.

Directions for Tag

1. Nuts may be poured into a serving dish right out of the jar, or they may be warmed 5 minutes in a 300 degrees F. oven.

Tijuana Tidbits Mix-in-a-Jar

Crunchy, spicy, and totally addictive - this fabulous blend of tortilla chips, popcorn, cereal, and nuts is the ultimate party mix. Best of all, the recipe makes a big batch!

Ingredients:

4	c. tortilla chips, broken into 1½-inch pcs.
3	c. Crispix cereal
1	bag (3-3½ oz.) microwave popcorn, popped (8-9 c.)
1	can mixed cocktail nuts (12 oz.)
½	c. light corn syrup
½	c. butter
½	c. brown sugar, firmly packed
1	Tbs. chili powder
⅛	tsp. ground cinnamon
⅛-¼	tsp. ground red pepper

Directions:

1. Preheat oven to 250 degrees F.
2. In large roasting pan, combine tortilla chips, cereal, popcorn, and nuts.
3. In small saucepan, combine corn syrup, butter, brown sugar, chili powder, cinnamon, and red pepper; heat to boiling.
4. Pour over cereal mixture in pan, stirring to coat.
5. Bake 1 hour, stirring every 20 minutes.
6. Remove from oven and turn onto sheet of waxed paper to cool.
7. When completely cool, place into gift jars for up to 2 weeks.

Yields: 18 cups

Directions for Tag

1.   Transfer snack mix to serving bowl and enjoy. Or, eat it right out of the jar!

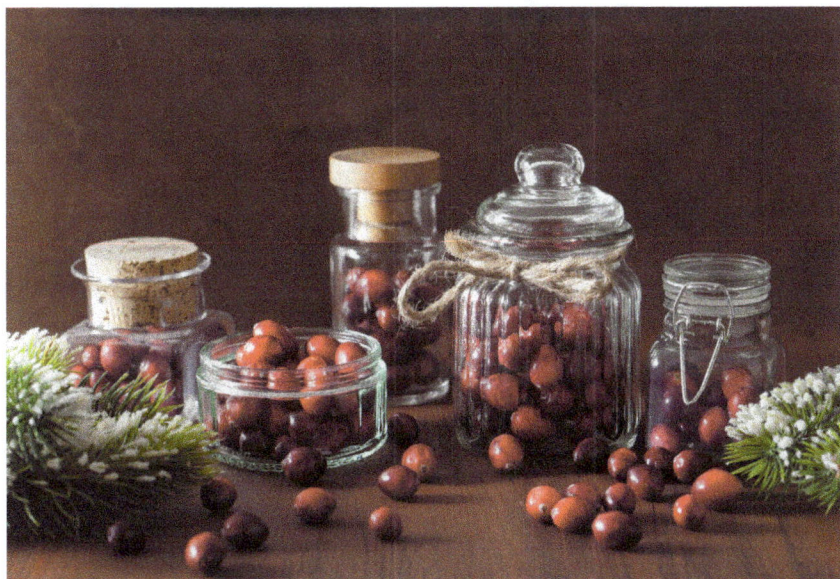

Vegetable Dip Mix-in-a-Jar

Vegetable dip is always popular during the holidays. This recipe has your gift recipient use tofu a nice healthy alternative.

Ingredients:

4	Tbs. dried parsley flakes
2	Tbs. plus 1 tsp. dried minced onion
2	tsp. garlic powder
1	tsp. dried dill or dried basil, optional
1	tsp. salt
¼	tsp. black pepper

Directions:

1. Mix ingredients and place in a jar.

Directions for Tag

Ingredients:

½	jar Vegetable Dip Mix
10½ oz.	tofu, soft silken, chilled
1-2	Tbs. vinegar or lemon juice

Directions:

1. In small bowl, blend Vegetable Dip Mix with tofu and vinegar /or/ lemon juice.
2. Serve with your favorite fresh vegetables.

Christmas Gifts-in-a-Jar Cookbook

A Collection of Christmas Gifts-in-a-Jar Recipes
Gifts-in-a-Jar Cookbook Series – Book 1

Beverages

Table of Contents

Café Bavarian Mint Flavored
Coffee Mix-in-a-Jar

Coffee lovers will enjoy this festive chocolate and mint flavored mix.

Ingredients:

¼	c. powdered creamer
⅓	c. sugar
¼	c. instant coffee
3	Tbs. powdered baking cocoa
3	hard candy peppermints

Directions:

1. Place ingredients into blender or food processor, blend until finely ground.
2. Store in airtight jar.

Directions for Tag

Directions:

1. Mix 1 to 2 tablespoons Café Bavarian Mint Flavored Coffee into 8 ounces hot water.
2. Enjoy!

Cafe Spiced Viennese Coffee Mix-in-a-Jar

This is a fragrant, flavored coffee that is easy to make and great for gift giving.

Ingredients:

⅔   c. instant coffee
⅔   c. sugar
¾   c. powdered nondairy creamer
½   tsp. cinnamon
⅛   tsp. nutmeg

Directions:

1.   Place ingredients into blender or food processor, blend until finely ground.
2.   Store in airtight jar.

Directions for Tag

1.   Mix 4 teaspoons Café Spiced Viennese Coffee into 8 ounces hot water.
2.   Enjoy!

Chai Mix-in-a-Jar

I love chai mix and this homemade version is very tasty and enjoyable. This makes a great gift for the tea enthusiast.

Ingredients:

1¼	c. nonfat dry milk powder
¼	c. black tea leaf
12	cardamom pod
4	cinnamon stick
2	tsp. dried lemon peel

Directions:

1. Divide ingredients, layering equally between two 6-ounce jars.

Directions for Tag

1. In large saucepan, place contents of one jar with 4 cups water; bring to boiling.
2. Remove from heat, let stand 5 minutes.
3. Strain through wire strainer lined with cheesecloth or coffee filter.
4. Add honey to taste.

Cherry Tea Mix-in-a-Jar

This is an easy mix for those who like cherry-flavored tea.

Ingredients:

1	pkg. cherry-flavored soft drink mix
1¼	c. instant tea mix

Directions:

1. In small bowl, combine ingredients until well blended.
2. Store in airtight container.

Yields: 1¼ cup mix.

Directions for Tag

1. Stir 2 teaspoons Cherry Tea Mix into 8 ounces hot or cold water.

Chocolate Mint Coffee Mix-in-a-Jar

This is a great drink and also makes a great gift. You can easily make this as a gift-in-a-jar recipe by layering the ingredients in a fancy quart jar and then including the directions on a gift tag.

Ingredients:

1	c. instant dry coffee
1	c. sugar
½	c. nonfat dry milk
1	c. nondairy creamer
½	c. baking cocoa
½	c. crushed peppermint candies

Directions:

1. In blender container, combine ingredients until consistency of fine powder.
2. Store mix in airtight containers.

Directions for Tag

1. Stir 1 to 2 tablespoons Chocolate Mint Coffee Mix into coffee mug of hot water.

Eggnog: Basic Non-Alcohol Mix-in-a-Jar

Eggnog made in dairies is usually pasteurized, which means that harmful bacteria have already been eliminated through a heating process. So when you whip up a batch of eggnog play it safe. Heat your eggs or buy it from a dairy and add your own finishing touches.

Ingredients:

12	eggs
1½	c. sugar, divided
1	qt. cream
	vanilla extract, to taste
	dash of nutmeg

Directions:

1. Separate eggs at room temperature.
2. In small bowl, beat yolks until creamed with half the sugar.
3. Beat whites until peaked, add other half of sugar.
4. Beat cream stiff; then fold all together.
5. Add vanilla, but remember a little bit of vanilla goes a long way.
6. Pour into jars and keep refrigerated.
7. Shake before serving.

Directions for Tag

1. Chill and keep refrigerated.
2. Use for the Eggless Eggnog Non-Alcohol recipe.

Eggless Eggnog, Non-Alcohol Mix-in-a-Jar

The French vanilla flavoring in the pudding in this recipe gives it a unique taste. For gift giving, you can give it as a powder mix in a jar or you can make it up and give it ready to be served.

Ingredients:

1	pkg. French vanilla instant pudding (3 oz.)
½	c. sugar
½	tsp. of nutmeg

Directions:

1. In medium bowl, mix all ingredients together.

Directions for Tag

Ingredients:

1	jar Non-Alcohol, Eggless Eggnog
8	c. milk
2	tsp. vanilla extract

Directions:

1. With electric mixer, beat 1 cup milk with contents of Non-Alcohol, Eggless Eggnog Mix until pudding is formed.
2. When pudding is formed, add remaining milk and vanilla; mix well.
3. In large jars, pour eggnog.
4. Chill and keep refrigerated.

Gingerbread Coffee Mix-in-a-Jar

Our family loves gingerbread, so this gingerbread-flavored coffee mix is a real treat.

Ingredients:

3	c. powdered creamer
1	c. dark brown sugar, packed
1	tsp. ground ginger
1	tsp. ground cinnamon
1	tsp. ground allspice
1	tsp. ground nutmeg
1	tsp. ground cloves
¾	c. instant coffee

Directions:

1. Place ingredients into food processor and blend until a fine powder.

Yields: 24 servings

Directions for Tag

1. Mix 2 heaping teaspoons or more of Gingerbread Coffee Mix with hot water in coffee mug.

Hot Chocolate Mix-in-a-Jar

I used to make this all the time on those cold winter days. The adults loved it as much as the kids! Adding the whipped cream and creamer and powdered sugar made such a difference and gave it such a rich taste!

Ingredients:

3	c. powdered milk
½	c. unsweetened cocoa powder
¼	c. sugar
½	c. powdered sugar
¼	c. powdered whipped cream
⅛	c. powdered creamer

Directions:

1. In large bowl, sift ingredients together.
2. Pack mix into airtight jar for storage.

Directions for Tag

Directions:

1. Spoon 2 to 4 tablespoons Hot Chocolate Mix into mug, pour hot water over and stir.
2. Enjoy!

Hot Malted Cocoa Mix-in-a-Jar

Our family loves malt. This particular recipe uses malted milk powder for that extra-special unique taste.

Ingredients:

1	pkg. nonfat dry milk powder (25.6 oz.)
6	c. miniature marshmallows
1	instant chocolate milk mix (16 oz.)
1	jar malted milk powder (13 oz.)
1	c. sifted powdered sugar
1	jar plain non-dairy powdered creamer (6 oz.)
½	tsp. salt

Directions:

1. In large bowl, combine ingredients and mix well.
2. Pour into 5 1-quart canning jars.
3. Seal and decorate, attach recipe tag.

Directions for Tag

1. Place ⅓ cup of Hot Malted Cocoa Mix into mug.
2. Pour in ¾ cup of hot water and stir well.

Instant Cocoa Mix-in-a-Jar for Diabetics

This recipe does not add any sugar so it can be used by diabetics or by those wishing to cut their sugar intake.

Ingredients:

2	c. nonfat dry milk powder
½	c. low-fat powdered nondairy creamer
½	c. unsweetened cocoa powder
10	pkts. Equal sweetener
¾	tsp. ground cinnamon

Directions:

1. Mix ingredients together and place in jar.

Yields: 2⅔ c. mix. (8 six-ounce servings)

Directions for Tag

1. Place ⅓ cup Instant Cocoa Mix into mug.
2. Pour in ¾ cup of hot water and stir well.

Irish Cream Coffee Creamer Mix-in-a-Jar

This flavored creamer adds a wonderful flavor to coffee.

Ingredients:

1	pkg. butter mints, crushed
2	c. chocolate malt powder
½	c. instant chocolate drink mix powder
2	c. non dairy powdered coffee creamer

Directions:

1. In blender container, combine ingredients until well blended.
2. Pour into airtight gift jar.

Directions for Tag

1. Add 1 heaping teaspoonful of Irish Cream Coffee Creamer Mix to your cup of coffee.
2. Enjoy!

Mexican Hot Chocolate Mix-in-a-Jar

Mexican hot chocolate has the addition of cinnamon and brown sugar for extra flavor.

Ingredients:

- ⅓   c. light brown sugar
- ¾   tsp. ground cinnamon
- 1½   tsp. powdered vanilla
- ¼   c. cocoa
- 2½   c. powdered milk

Directions:

1. In small bowl, combine all ingredients; blend well.
2. Store in airtight jar decorated with pretty ribbon.

Directions for Tag

Ingredients:

- 3   c. hot water
  Mexican Hot Chocolate Mix, to taste
  cinnamon sticks for garnish

Directions:

1. In medium saucepan, heat water to boiling.
2. Add Mexican Hot Chocolate Mix, stir with whisk until mixture is smooth.
3. Garnish with cinnamon sticks.
4. For a frothier hot chocolate, mix in blender.

Yields: 6 servings.

Mocha Cooler Mix-in-a-Jar

This mocha mix will delight those looking for a unique cool drink to quench their thirst.

Ingredients:

¼	c. instant coffee granules
1	c. sugar
1	c. dry milk
1	c. dry coffee creamer
⅛	tsp. salt

Directions:

1. With rolling pin, crush coffee granules into fine powder.
2. In small bowl, mix all ingredients together.
3. Pour into jar and tightly seal.

Yields: 7 batches.

Directions for Tag

Ingredients:

1½	c. crushed ice
½	c. milk
½	c. Mocha Cooler Mix
	whipped topping

Directions:

1. In blender container, combine ice, milk, and Mocha Cooler Mix.
2. Blend on high until smooth.
3. Pour into glasses, top with whipped topping.

Orange Cappuccino Coffee Mix-in-a-Jar

Coffee lovers will delight in this simple coffee that is unique with the flavor of dried orange peel and cinnamon.

Ingredients:

½	c. instant coffee granules
½	tsp. grated dried orange peel
1	c. nondairy powdered coffee creamer
¾	c. sugar
½	tsp. ground cinnamon

Directions:

1. In blender container or food processor, finely grind coffee and orange peel.
2. Add remaining ingredients and process until well blended.
3. Store in airtight jar decorated with ribbon.

Yields: 1⅔ cups coffee mix.

Directions for Tag

1. Put 1 heaping tablespoon Orange Cappuccino Coffee Mix into coffee mug.
2. Pour in hot water and stir.
3. Put your feet up and enjoy!

Orange Float Mix-in-a-Jar

This is another cool drink mix that is easy to make that makes an attractive gift when put in a decorative jar with a gift tag.

Ingredients:

4	c. instant nonfat dry milk
2	c. powdered orange drink mix
1	c. sugar

Directions:

1. In large bowl, combine all ingredients and blend well.
2. Place in gift jar and store in cool dry place.

Yields: 7 cups.

Directions for Tag

1. To make orange float, add ½ cup of Orange Float Mix to 8 ounces of cold water in a blender.
2. Add 2 to 3 ice cubes and blend well.
3. Enjoy!

Orange Spiced Tea Mix-in-a-Jar

This mix also adds some color inside your decorative jar. It makes a soothing hot drink to soothe your throat.

Ingredients:

1	jar sugar free iced tea mix with lemon (3.3 oz)
2	pkg. sugar-free orange breakfast drink mix (1.8 oz)
1	Tbs. plus 1 tsp. ground cinnamon
2	tsp. ground cloves

Directions:

1. In small bowl, combine all ingredients.
2. Package into 3 1-cup gift jars.

Directions for Tag

1. Stir in 1½ teaspoon of mixture into 1 cup hot water.
2. There are only 3 calories per 1 cup serving. 0 fat, 0 cholesterol, and 1 milligram sodium.
3. Enjoy!

Peach Tea Mix-in-a Jar

This tea is flavored with peach for a fragrant spiced tea mix.

Ingredients:

    1   c. instant tea mix
    1   box peach gelatin powder (3 oz.)
    2   c. sugar

Directions:

    1.   In medium bowl, combine all ingredients; mix well.
    2.   Store in airtight jar.

Yields: 3½ cups.

Directions for Tag

    1.   Combine 2 teaspoons Peach Tea Mix with 8 ounces hot water.

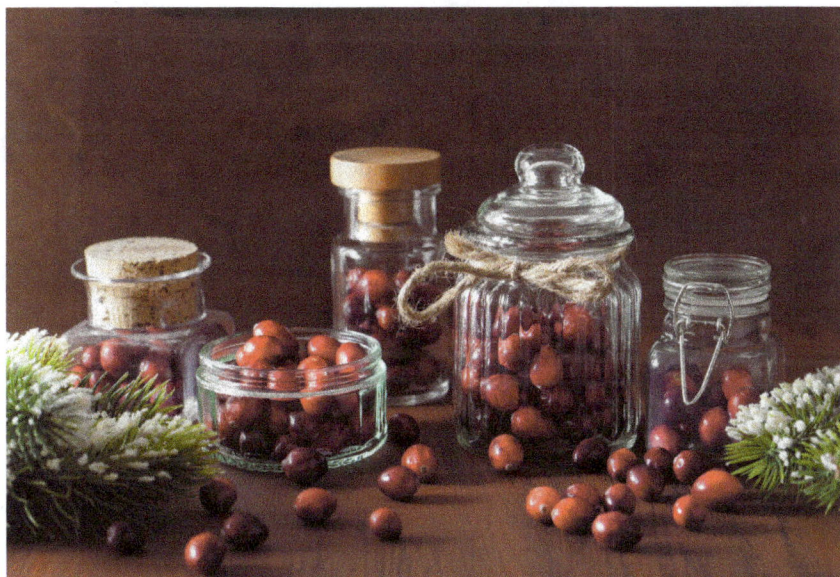

Red Hot Sipper Mix-in-a-Jar

Cinnamon candies add color and variety to this spiced tea mix that your gift recipients will be sure to enjoy.

Ingredients:

- 1⅔   c. instant powdered lemon flavor tea mix
- 2   Tbs. instant powdered orange pineapple sweetened drink mix
- 5   Tbs. red hot cinnamon candies

Directions:

1. In small bowl, combine tea drink mix and orange pineapple drink mix; place mixture into pint jar.
2. Layer red hot cinnamon candies on top of drink mix.

Yields: 16 cups.

Directions for Tag

1. Measure 2 tablespoons Red Hot Sipper drink mix into drinking mug.
2. Pour 1 cup of hot water over drink mixture.
3. Stir until well-blended and red hot cinnamon candies are melted.

Spiced Cranberry Cider Mix-in-a-Jar

Dried cranberries and fresh cinnamon sticks, along with cloves and allspice, make a fragrant gift. Be sure to use the freshest spices you can find for an attractive flavorful drink.

Ingredients:

½	c. dried cranberries
12	cinnamon sticks
½	tsp. whole cloves, crushed
2	Tbs. whole allspice

Directions:

1. In small bowl, stir cranberries and spices together.
2. Store in airtight gift jars.

Yields: 12 to 14 servings.

Directions for Tag

Ingredients:

2	qt. apple cider
1	qt. water
1	jar Spiced Cranberry Cider Mix
2	oranges, sliced

Directions:

1. In large saucepan, combine cider, water, and Spiced Cranberry Cider Mix.
2. Heat mixture, but do not boil.
3. Add most of orange slices. Serve warm.
4. Garnish with remaining orange slices.

Spiced Tea Mix-in-a-Jar

This makes a quick and easy mix for gift giving.

Ingredients:

1	powdered orange breakfast drink (9 oz.)
1	powdered lemon flavored ice tea drink (4 oz.)
1½	c. sugar
3	tsp. ground cinnamon
2	tsp. ground cloves
1	tsp. ground ginger

Directions:

1. In large jar, blend together orange drink powder, lemon ice tea powder, sugar, and spices.
2. Label and store tightly covered in decorated jars at room temperature, no longer than 6 months.

Yields: 5½ cups mix.

Directions for Tag

1. For each serving mix 3 teaspoons spiced tea mix and 1 cup hot water together in a mug until mix is dissolved.
2. Garnish each with a twist of lemon or orange peel and a cinnamon stick if desired.

Toffee Coffee Mix-in-a-Jar

Our family loves toffee. The toffee flavor in this coffee mix can be made simply by combining brown sugar with instant coffee and creamer. Feel free to use either light or dark brown sugar for a delightful drink.

Ingredients:

⅔   c. instant coffee
1   c. nondairy creamer
1   c. brown sugar

Directions:

1. In medium bowl, combine all ingredients.
2. Place in airtight jars.

Directions for Tag

1. Place 2 to 3 teaspoons of Toffee Coffee Mix into mug and add hot water.

Christmas Gifts-in-a-Jar Cookbook
A Collection of Christmas Gifts-in-a-Jar Recipes
Gifts-in-a-Jar Cookbook Series – Book 1

Breads and Muffins

Table of Contents

Apricot Bread Mix-in-a-Jar

Our family loves apricots, and this not only makes tasty bread, it is also a lovely gift.

Ingredients for bread mix:

2½	c. quick biscuit mix
½	c. sugar
1	tsp. baking powder
¼	tsp. salt
¾	c. dried apricots, chopped
¾	c. nuts

Directions:

1. Layer in 1-quart wide-mouth (makes it easier to pack down) canning jar in order listed above.
2. After each layer, pack the layer down.
3. Copy instructions and attach to jar.

Directions for Tag

Additional Ingredients:

1	jar Apricot Bread Mix
1¼	c. milk
1	tsp. vanilla extract
2	eggs, slightly beaten
½	c. butter, softened

Directions:

1. Preheat oven to 350 degrees F.
2. Lightly grease a large loaf pan.
3. In large bowl, mix ingredients of jar together with milk, vanilla, eggs, and butter.
4. Mix until completely blended.

5. Pour batter into prepared loaf pan.
6. Bake 1 hour or until wooden toothpick inserted in center comes out clean.
7. Cool in pan on wire rack before removing.

Apricot-Walnut Muffin Mix-in-a-Jar

Apricots and walnuts provide the perfect flavor combination to these muffins. Enjoy!

Ingredients:

1½	c. all-purpose flour
2	tsp. baking powder
¼	tsp. baking soda
¼	tsp. salt
1	c. oatmeal
½	c. brown sugar, packed
½	c. dried apricots, chopped
⅓	c. walnuts, chopped

Directions:

1. Starting with first ingredient, layer ingredients into clean, dry 1-quart wide-mouth jar in order given.
2. Press each layer firmly with flat-bottomed object, making layers as level as possible.
3. Secure lid, label, and store in cool dry place for up to 12 months.
4. For gift giving, decorate lid as desired.
5. Copy instructions attach to jar.

Yields: 1 quart jar.

Directions for Tag

Additional Ingredients:

1	jar Apricot-Walnut Muffin Mix
1	c. milk
¼	c. melted butter, slightly cooled
1	egg, slightly beaten

Directions:

1. Preheat oven to 375 degrees F.
2. Lightly grease or paper line muffin tin(s); set aside.
3. In large bowl, cream milk, butter, and egg together.
4. Add contents of jar; stir until just mixed. (Do not over mix).
5. Spoon batter into prepared muffin tin(s), filling each cup ⅔ full.
6. Bake 20 to 25 minutes or until wooden toothpick inserted in center of muffin comes out clean.
7. Cool 10 minutes in tin, remove, and cool completely.
8. Store in airtight container for up to 1 week.

Yields: 12 muffins.

Blueberry Bread Mix-in-a-Jar

This mix in a jar provides the base for a quick bread that is great fresh out of the oven.

Ingredients:

2½	c. biscuit mix
¼	tsp. salt
1	tsp. baking powder
½	c. sugar
½	c. dried blueberries
1	c. walnuts, chopped

Directions:

1. Starting with first ingredient, layer ingredients into clean, dry 1-quart wide-mouth jar in order given; press each layer firmly with flat-bottomed object, making layers as level as possible.
2. Secure lid, label, and store in cool dry place for up to 12 months.
3. For gift giving, decorate lid as desired.
4. Copy instructions and attach to jar.

Yields: 1 quart jar.

Directions for Tag

Additional Ingredients:

1	jar Blueberry Bread Mix
1¼	c. buttermilk
½	c. butter, softened
1	tsp. vanilla extract
2	eggs, slightly beaten

Directions:

1. Preheat oven to 350 degrees F.
2. Lightly grease a 9 x 5-inch loaf pan.
3. In large bowl, cream buttermilk, butter, vanilla, and eggs together.
4. Add contents of jar; stir until just mixed. (Do not over mix).
5. Pour batter into prepared loaf pan.
6. Bake 50 to 55 minutes or until wooden toothpick inserted in center of loaf comes out clean.
7. Cool 10 minutes in pan, remove bread, and cool completely on wire rack.
8. Store in airtight container for up to 1 week.

Yields: 1 loaf.

Blueberry-Apricot Streusel Bread
Mix-in-a-Jar

Blueberries and apricots combine to make a colorful mix. The streusel topping add the perfect crunch and flavor.

Ingredients for bread:

2	c. all-purpose flour
1	tsp. baking powder
½	tsp. baking soda
½	tsp. salt
1	c. sugar
¾	c. dried apricots, chopped
¾	c. dried blueberries, chopped

Ingredients for topping:

2	Tbs. all-purpose flour
2	Tbs. sugar
2	Tbs. sliced almonds, chopped
1	tsp. ground cinnamon

Directions:

1. In medium bowl, combine flour, baking powder, soda, and salt; stir well.
2. Pour into clean, dry 1-quart wide-mouth jar; pack down well with flat-bottomed object.
3. Add sugar, apricots, and blueberries in order given.
4. Press each layer firmly, making layers as level as possible.
5. In small plastic food storage bag, blend topping ingredients; force air from bag before sealing.
6. Close with twist tie and cut off excess; place in jar.
7. Secure lid, label, and store in cool, dry place.
8. For gift giving, decorate lid as desired.
9. Copy instructions and attach to jar.

Directions for Tag

Additional Ingredients:

1	jar Blueberry-Apricot Streusel Bread Mix
½	c. unsalted butter, melted and cooled
¾	c. buttermilk
1	lg. egg, beaten
1	tsp. vanilla extract
1	tsp. almond extract
2	Tbs. cold unsalted butter, cut into pcs.

Directions:

1. Preheat oven to 350 degrees F.
2. Lightly grease a 9 x 5-inch loaf pan; set aside.
3. Remove bag from jar; set aside.
4. In large bowl, pour remaining contents of jar; mix well.
5. Make well in center of dry ingredients.
6. In medium bowl, combine melted butter, buttermilk, egg, vanilla, and almond extract; mix well.
7. Add to dry ingredients; stir only until dry ingredients are moistened.
8. Pour batter into prepared loaf pan.
9. For topping, pour contents of bag into small bowl.
10. Add 2 tablespoons butter pieces, and press into dry ingredients with fork until mixture is crumbly.
11. Sprinkle evenly over batter.
12. Bake 55 to 60 minutes or until wooden toothpick inserted in center comes out clean.
13. Cool 15 minutes in pan, transfer to wire rack to cool completely.
14. Store in airtight container.

Butter Pecan Bread Mix-in-a-Jar

This rich, buttery bread is flavored with pecans, brown sugar, and cinnamon.

Ingredients:

2¼	c. all-purpose flour
2	tsp. baking powder
½	tsp. salt
½	tsp. baking soda
¼	tsp. ground nutmeg
½	tsp. ground cinnamon
1	c. brown sugar, packed
1	c. pecans, chopped

Directions:

1. Starting with first ingredient, layer ingredients into clean, dry 1-quart wide-mouth jar in order given; press each layer firmly with flat-bottomed object, making layers as level as possible.
2. Secure lid, label, and store in cool dry place for up to 12 months.
3. For gift giving, decorate lid as desired.
4. Copy instructions and attach to jar.

Yields: 1 quart jar.

Directions for Tag

Additional Ingredients:

1	jar Butter Pecan Bread Mix
1	c. buttermilk
2	Tbs. butter, softened
1	egg, slightly beaten

Directions:

1. Preheat oven to 350 degrees F.
2. Lightly grease a 9 x 5-inch loaf pan.
3. In large bowl, cream buttermilk, butter, and egg.
4. Add contents of jar; stir until just mixed. (Do not over mix).
5. Pour batter into prepared loaf pan.
6. Bake 50 to 55 minutes or until wooden toothpick inserted in center of loaf comes out clean.
7. Cool 10 minutes in pan, remove bread, and cool completely on wire rack.
8. Store in airtight container for up to 1 week.

Yields: 1 loaf.

Cherry Pumpkin Nut Bread Mix-in-a-Jar

Dried cherries add a colorful and festive surprise to this moist pumpkin bread. This makes a colorful Christmas gift.

Ingredients:

1⅔	c. all-purpose flour
1	tsp. baking soda
½	tsp. salt
¾	c. white sugar
⅓	c. brown sugar, firmly packed
1½	tsp. ground cinnamon
1	tsp. ground cloves, or more to taste
1	tsp. ground nutmeg
1	c. walnuts, chopped
1	c. dried cherries, chopped

Directions:

1. In medium bowl, combine flour, soda, and salt; stir well.
2. Pour into clean, dry 1-quart wide-mouth jar; pack down well with flat-bottomed object.
3. Add white sugar and pack down.
4. Combine brown sugar, cinnamon, cloves, and nutmeg; add to jar and pack down.
5. Add walnuts and cherries; pack down lightly after each layer.
6. Secure lid, label, and store in cool, dry place.
7. For gift giving, decorate lid as desired.
8. Copy instructions and attach to jar.

Yields: 1 quart jar.

Directions for Tag

Additional Ingredients:

1	jar Cherry Pumpkin Nut Bread Mix
1¼	c. solid-pack pumpkin
1	egg, lightly beaten
¼	c. canola oil

Directions:

1. Preheat oven to 350 degrees F.
2. Lightly grease a 9 x 5-inch loaf pan; set aside.
3. In large bowl, pour contents of jar; mix well.
4. Make well in center of dry ingredients.
5. In medium bowl, combine pumpkin, egg, and oil; mix well.
6. Add to dry ingredients; stir only until ingredients are moistened.
7. Pour batter into prepared loaf pan.
8. Bake 45 to 55 minutes or until wooden toothpick inserted in center comes out clean.
9. Cool 15 minutes in pan, transfer to wire rack to cool completely.
10. Store in airtight container.

Yields: 1 loaf.

Chocolate Chip Banana Bread
Mix-in-a-Jar

My children have always loved chocolate chips in their banana bread and this will make a welcome treat.

Ingredients:

2½	c. biscuit mix
¼	tsp. salt
1	tsp. baking powder
½	c. sugar
½	c. dried bananas, coarsely chopped
1	c. chocolate chips

Directions:

1. Starting with first ingredient, layer ingredients into clean, dry 1-quart wide-mouth jar in order given; press each layer firmly with flat-bottomed object, making layers as level as possible.
2. Secure lid, label, and store in cool dry place for up to 12 months.
3. For gift giving, decorate lid as desired.
4. Copy instructions and attach to jar.

Yields: 1 quart jar.

Directions for Tag

Additional Ingredients:

1	jar Chocolate Chip Banana Bread Mix
1¼	c. buttermilk
½	c. butter, softened
2	eggs, slightly beaten
1	tsp. vanilla extract

Directions:

1. Preheat oven to 350 degrees F.
2. Lightly grease a 9 x 5-inch loaf pan.
3. In large bowl, cream buttermilk, butter, eggs, and vanilla.
4. Add contents of jar; stir until just mixed. (Do not over mix).
5. Pour batter into prepared loaf pan.
6. Bake 50 to 55 minutes or until wooden toothpick inserted in center of loaf comes out clean.
7. Cool 10 minutes in pan, remove bread, and cool completely on wire rack.
8. Store in airtight container for up to 1 week.

Yields: 1 loaf.

Chocolate Chip Raisin Bread
Mix-in-a-Jar

Raisins and walnuts add texture and taste to this quick bread. Enjoy!

Ingredients:

2½   c. biscuit mix
¼   tsp. salt
1   tsp. baking powder
½   c. sugar
½   c. walnuts, chopped
½   c. raisins
1   c. chocolate chips

Directions:

1. Starting with first ingredient, layer ingredients into clean, dry 1-quart wide-mouth jar in order given.
2. Press each layer firmly with flat-bottomed object, making layers as level as possible.
3. Secure lid, label, and store in cool dry place for up to 12 months.
4. For gift giving, decorate lid as desired.
5. Copy instructions and attach to jar.

Yields: 1 quart jar.

Directions for Tag

Additional Ingredients:

1   jar Chocolate Chip Raisin Bread Mix
1¼   c. buttermilk
½   c. butter, softened
2   eggs, slightly beaten
1   tsp. vanilla extract

Directions:

1. Preheat oven to 350 degrees F.
2. Lightly grease a 9 x 5-inch loaf pan.
3. In large bowl cream buttermilk, butter, eggs, and vanilla.
4. Add contents of jar; stir until just mixed. (Do not over mix).
5. Pour batter into prepared loaf pan.
6. Bake 50 to 55 minutes or until wooden toothpick inserted in center of loaf comes out clean.
7. Cool 10 minutes in pan, remove bread, and cool completely on wire rack.
8. Store in airtight container for up to 1 week.

Yields: 1 loaf.

Cranberry Chocolate-Chunk Muffin Mix-in-a-Jar

Give a gift that will provide a great addition to your family member and friends. The cranberries add Christmas color to these moist muffins.

Ingredients:

¾   c. toasted pecans, coarsely chopped
2   c. all-purpose flour
2   tsp. baking powder
½   tsp. salt
½   c. sugar
½   c. dried cranberries, coarsely chopped
4   oz. semisweet chocolate bar, chopped into ½-in. chunks (about ¾ cup)

Directions for toasting pecans:

1.   In heavy-bottomed skillet, spread pecans in single layer.
2.   Cook over medium heat 1 to 2 minutes, stirring frequently, until pecans are lightly browned.
3.   Remove from skillet immediately.
4.   Cool before using.

Directions for mix:

1.   In medium bowl, combine flour, baking powder, and salt; stir well.
2.   Pour into clean, dry 1-quart wide-mouth jar; pack down well.
3.   Add sugar, cranberries, pecans, and chocolate; press each layer firmly with flat-bottomed object, making layers as level as possible.
4.   Secure lid, label, and store in cool, dry place.
5.   For gift giving, decorate lid as desired.
6.   Copy instructions and attach to jar.

Directions for Tag

Additional Ingredients:

1	jar Cranberry Chocolate-Chunk Muffin Mix
½	c. orange juice
½	c. canola oil
2	lg. eggs, lightly beaten
¾	tsp. orange extract

Directions:

1. Preheat oven to 375 degrees F.
2. Lightly grease or paper line muffin tin(s); set aside.
3. In large bowl, pour contents of jar; stir until ingredients are evenly mixed, make well in center.
4. In small bowl, combine juice, oil, eggs, and orange extract; mix well.
5. Add to dry ingredients; stir just until moistened.
6. Spoon batter into prepared muffin tin(s), filling each cup half full.
7. Bake 18 to 22 minutes or until wooden toothpick inserted into center comes out clean.
8. Cool 5 minutes in pan on wire rack.
9. Transfer muffins to wire rack.
10. Serve warm.
11. Store in airtight container.

Yields: 12 muffins.

Eggnog Cherry Quick Bread
Mix-in-a-Jar

Christmas is a time to enjoy eggnog and the addition of cherries makes a colorful Christmas treat.

Ingredients:

2¼	c. all-purpose flour, divided
1	Tbs. baking powder
½	tsp. salt
1	tsp. ground nutmeg
¾	c. sugar
½	c. candied or dried cherries, chopped
¾	c. pecans, chopped

Directions:

1. In medium bowl, combine 1½ cups flour, baking powder, and salt; stir well.
2. Pour into clean, dry 1-quart wide-mouth jar; pack down well with flat-bottomed object.
3. Combine remaining ¾ cup flour and nutmeg; add to jar and pack down.
4. Add sugar, cherries, and pecans.
5. Press each layer lightly, making layers as level as possible.
6. Secure lid, label, and store in cool, dry place.
7. For gift giving, decorate lid as desired.
8. Copy instructions and attach to jar.

Yields: 1 quart jar.

Directions for Tag

Additional Ingredients:

1	jar Eggnog Cherry Quick Bread Mix
1¼	c. prepared dairy eggnog or half-and-half
2	eggs, slightly beaten
6	Tbs. butter, melted and cooled
1	tsp. vanilla extract

Directions:

1. Preheat oven to 350 degrees F.
2. Lightly grease 3 miniature (5½ x 3-inch) loaf pans or one 9 x 5-inch loaf pan; set aside.
3. In large bowl, pour contents of jar; mix well.
4. Make well in center of dry ingredients.
5. In medium bowl, combine eggnog, eggs, butter, and vanilla; mix well.
6. Add to dry ingredients; stir only until dry ingredients are moistened.
7. Pour batter in prepared pans.
8. Bake 35 to 40 minutes or until wooden toothpick inserted in center comes out clean.
9. Cool 15 minutes in pans, transfer to wire rack to cool completely.
10. Store in airtight container.

Yields: 3 miniature loaves or 1 standard loaf.

Ginger Spice Muffin Mix-in-a-Jar

These muffins are moist and flavorful.

Ingredients:

¼	tsp. ground cloves
¼	tsp. ground ginger
½	tsp. ground nutmeg
1	tsp. ground cinnamon
½	tsp. salt
2	tsp. baking powder
½	c. sugar
1¾	c. all-purpose flour

Directions:

1. Starting with first ingredient, layer ingredients into clean, dry 1-pint wide-mouth jar in order given.
2. Press each layer firmly with flat-bottomed object, making layers as level as possible.
3. Secure lid, label, and store in cool dry place for up to 12 months.
4. For gift giving, decorate lid as desired.
5. Copy instructions and attach to jar.

Yields: 1 pint jar.

Directions for Tag

Additional Ingredients:

1	jar Ginger Spice Muffin Mix
1	c. milk
¼	c. melted butter, slightly cooled
1	egg, slightly beaten
1	tsp. vanilla extract

Directions:

1. Preheat oven to 400 degrees F.
2. Lightly grease or paper line muffin tin(s).
3. In large bowl, cream milk, butter, egg, and vanilla.
4. Add contents of jar; stir until just mixed. (Do not over mix).
5. Spoon batter into prepared muffin tin(s), filling each cup ⅔ full.
6. Bake 15 to 20 minutes or until wooden toothpick inserted in center of muffin comes out clean.
7. Cool 10 minutes in tin, remove, and cool completely.
8. Store in airtight container for up to 1 week.

Yields: 12 muffins.

Golden Cornbread Mix-in-a-Jar

Cornbread goes well with a bowl of chili. This easy cornbread is a real treat topped with butter and honey.

Ingredients:

1	Tbs. baking powder
½	c. sugar
½	c. cornmeal
1¼	c. biscuit mix

Directions:

1. Starting with first ingredient, layer ingredients into clean, dry 1-pint wide-mouth jar in order given; press each layer firmly with flat-bottomed object, making layers as level as possible.
2. Secure lid, label, and store in cool dry place for up to 12 months.
3. For gift giving, decorate lid as desired.
4. Copy instructions and attach to jar.

Yields: 1 pint jar.

Directions for Tag

Additional Ingredients:

1	jar Golden Cornbread Mix
1	c. milk
½	c. butter, melted, slightly cooled
2	eggs, slightly beaten

Directions:

1. Preheat oven to 350 degrees F.
2. Lightly grease a 9-inch round cake pan.
3. In large bowl, cream milk, butter, and eggs together.
4. Add contents of jar; stir until just mixed. (Do not over mix).
5. Pour batter into prepared cake pan.
6. Bake 30 to 35 minutes or until wooden toothpick inserted in center of cornbread comes out clean.
7. Cool completely before cutting into wedges.
8. Store in airtight container for up to 1 week.

Yields: 8 servings.

Golden Pecan Muffin Mix-in-a-Jar

These delicious muffins go great with your favorite cup of coffee.

Ingredients:

½	tsp. salt
½	tsp. ground cinnamon
2	tsp. baking powder
½	c. sugar
1½	c. all-purpose flour
½	c. pecans, chopped

Directions:

1. Starting with first ingredient, layer ingredients into clean, dry 1-pint wide-mouth jar in order given.
2. Press each layer firmly with flat-bottomed object, making layers as level as possible.
3. Secure lid, label, and store in cool dry place for up to 12 months.
4. For gift giving, decorate lid as desired.
5. Copy instructions and attach to jar.

Yields: 1 pint jar.

Directions for Tag

Additional Ingredients:

1	jar Golden Pecan Muffin Mix
½	c. milk
¼	c. canola oil
1	egg, slightly beaten

Directions:

1. Preheat oven to 400 degrees F.
2. Lightly grease or paper line muffin tin(s).
3. In large bowl, blend milk, oil, and egg.
4. Add contents of jar; stir until just mixed. (Do not over mix).
5. Spoon batter into prepared muffin tin(s), filling each cup half full.
6. Bake 15 to 18 minutes or until wooden toothpick inserted in center of muffin comes out clean.
7. Cool 10 minutes in tin, remove, and cool completely.
8. Store in airtight container for up to 1 week.

Yields: 12 muffins

Nutty Cranberry Bread Mix-in-a-Jar

Nuts and cranberries make a great combination for a holiday gift but it is also delicious year round. Enjoy!

Ingredients:

2½	c. biscuit mix
¼	tsp. salt
1	tsp. baking powder
½	c. sugar
½	c. dried cranberries
1	c. walnuts, chopped

Directions:

1. Starting with first ingredient, layer ingredients into clean, dry 1-quart wide-mouth jar in order given.
2. Press each layer firmly with flat-bottomed object, making layers as level as possible.
3. Secure lid, label, and store in cool dry place for up to 12 months.
4. For gift giving, decorate lid as desired.
5. Copy instructions and attach to jar.

Yields: 1 quart jar.

Directions for Tag

Additional Ingredients:

1	jar Nutty Cranberry Bread Mix
1¼	c. buttermilk
½	c. butter, softened
1	tsp. vanilla extract
2	eggs, slightly beaten

Directions:

1. Preheat oven to 350 degrees F.
2. Lightly grease a 9 x 5-inch loaf pan.
3. In large bowl, cream buttermilk, butter, vanilla, and eggs together.
4. Add contents of jar; stir until just mixed. (Do not over mix).
5. Pour batter into prepared loaf pan.
6. Bake 50 to 55 minutes or until wooden toothpick inserted in center of loaf comes out clean.
7. Cool 10 minutes in pan, remove bread, and cool completely on wire rack.
8. Store in airtight container for up to 1 week.

Yields: 1 loaf.

Pumpkin Spice Mini Muffin Mix-in-a-Jar

These moist muffins will fill the kitchen with a fragrant aroma. Enjoy!

Ingredients:

2	c. all-purpose flour
2	tsp. baking powder
¾	tsp. salt
½	tsp. baking soda
½	c. brown sugar, packed
½	tsp. ground ginger
¼	tsp. ground nutmeg
¼	tsp. ground cloves
¾	c. dried cranberries, chopped
¼	c. sugar
1	tsp. ground cinnamon

Directions:

1. In medium bowl, combine flour, baking powder, salt, and soda; stir well.
2. Pour into clean, dry 1-quart wide-mouth jar; pack down well.
3. Combine brown sugar, ginger, nutmeg, and cloves; stir well.
4. Add to jar and pack down well.
5. Add cranberries and pack down.
6. In small plastic food storage bag, blend sugar and cinnamon; close with twist tie and cut off excess.
7. Place in jar; secure lid, label, and store in cool, dry place.
8. For gift giving, decorate lid as desired.
9. Copy instructions and attach to jar.

Yields: 1 quart jar.

Directions for Tag

Additional Ingredients:

1	jar pumpkin Spice Mini Muffin Mix
½	c. butter, softened
1	c. solid-pack pumpkin
2	eggs
½	c. orange juice
1	tsp. vanilla extract

Directions:

1. Preheat oven to 400 degrees F.
2. Lightly grease or paper line a 36-cup mini muffin tin or 12-cup muffin tin; set aside.
3. In small bowl, empty bag from jar; set aside.
4. In large bowl, pour contents of jar; stir until ingredients are evenly mixed.
5. In medium bowl, beat butter with electric mixer at medium speed until creamy.
6. Beat in pumpkin, eggs, orange juice, and vanilla until well blended (mixture may appear curdled).
7. Add to dry ingredients; stir just until moistened.
8. Pour batter into prepared muffin tin(s), filling each cup half full.
9. Bake 12 to 15 minutes or until wooden toothpick inserted in center comes out clean.
10. Transfer muffins to wire rack.
11. In small bowl, roll warm muffins in sugar mixture.
12. Serve warm.

Yields: 36 mini muffins or 12 standard muffins.

Raisin Bran Muffin Mix-in-a-Jar

These muffins, full of fiber and flavor, make a great start for the day.

Ingredients:

½	c. sugar
1¼	c. self-rising flour
1	c. dark raisins
1½	c. bran flakes

Directions:

1. Starting with first ingredient, layer ingredients into clean, dry 1-quart wide-mouth jar in order given; press each layer firmly with flat-bottomed object, making layers as level as possible.
2. Secure lid, label, and store in cool dry place for up to 12 months.
3. For gift giving, decorate lid as desired.
4. Copy instructions and attach to jar.

Yields: 1 quart jar.

Directions for Tag

Additional Ingredients:

1	jar Raisin Bran Muffin Mix
½	c. milk
½	c. melted butter, slightly cooled
1	egg, slightly beaten

Directions:

1. Preheat oven to 400 degrees F.
2. Lightly grease or paper line muffin tin(s).
3. In large bowl, cream milk, butter, and egg.
4. Add contents of jar; stir until just mixed. (Do not over mix).
5. Pour batter into prepared muffin tin(s), filling each cup half full.
6. Bake 15 to 18 minutes or until wooden toothpick inserted in center of muffin comes out clean.
7. Cool 10 minutes in tin, remove, and cool completely.
8. Store in airtight container for up to 1 week.

Yields: 12 muffins

Red, White, and Blue Muffin
Mix-in-a-Jar

Colorful ingredients add great flavors to this muffin mix in a jar.

Ingredients:

2	c. all-purpose flour
1	Tbs. baking powder
½	tsp. salt
½	c. sugar
¾	c. dried sweetened cranberries
¾	c. white chocolate chips
¾	c. dried blueberries

Directions:

1. In medium bowl, combine flour, baking powder, and salt; stir well.
2. Pour into clean, dry 1-quart wide-mouth jar; pack down well.
3. Add sugar, cranberries, chocolate chips, and blueberries in order given.
4. Press each layer firmly with flat-bottomed object, making layers as level as possible.
5. Secure lid, label, and store in cool, dry place.
6. For gift giving, decorate lid as desired.
7. Copy instructions and attach to jar.

Yields: 1 quart jar.

Directions for Tag

Additional Ingredients:

1	jar Red, White, and Blue Muffin Mix
1	c. milk
½	c. butter, melted and cooled
1	egg beaten
1	tsp. vanilla extract

Directions:

1. Preheat oven to 350 degrees F.
2. Lightly grease or paper line muffin tin(s); set aside.
3. In large bowl, combine milk, butter, egg, and vanilla.
4. Add contents of jar; stir just until moistened.
5. Pour batter into prepared muffin tin(s), filling each cup half full.
6. Bake 20 to 25 minutes or until wooden toothpick inserted in center comes out clean.
7. Transfer muffins to wire rack to cool 10 minutes.
8. Serve warm or at room temperature.

Yields: 12 muffins.

Christmas Gifts-in-a-Jar Cookbook
A Collection of Christmas Gifts-in-a-Jar Recipes
Gifts-in-a-Jar Cookbook Series – Book 1

Breakfasts

Table of Contents

Page

Apple/Cinnamon, Walnut, Oatmeal Mix-in-a-Jar

This makes an easy variation to breakfast oatmeal. Enjoy this for a busy morning meal.

Ingredients:

1	pkg. dried apples, finely chopped (7 oz.)
1	ctn. of oats, blended to smaller size (18 oz.)
1	jar non dairy creamer (3 oz.)
½	c. brown sugar
½	c. walnuts, chopped
1	tsp. salt
2	tsp. ground cinnamon

Directions:

1. Use clean, dry 1-quart wide-mouth canning jar.
2. In large bowl, mix all ingredients together, pour into jar.
3. Seal and decorate, attach recipe tag.

Directions for Tag

Additional Ingredients:

½	c. Apple/Cinnamon, Walnut, Oatmeal Mix
⅔	c. boiling water

Directions:

1. Mix until well blended.
2. Let thicken by sitting mixture aside a few minutes.
3. Eat as is or this may also be added to ingredients when you make pancakes!

Apple/Peach Oatmeal Mix-in-a-Jar

Try this breakfast oatmeal which has an interesting blend of flavors and is a welcome treat.

Ingredients:

2½	c. quick oats
½	c. freeze-dried peaches
½	c. non fat dry milk
1	tsp. chicken broth powder
⅓	c. sugar
2	tsp. almond flavoring, powdered
¼	tsp. ground cinnamon
¼	c. slivered almonds, chopped

Directions:

1. Use clean, dry 1-quart wide-mouth canning jar.
2. Layer ingredients in order given into jar.
3. Seal and decorate, attach recipe tag.

Directions for Tag

Additional Ingredients:

½	c. Apple/Peach Oatmeal Mix
⅔	c. boiling water

Directions:

1. In small bowl, mix until well blended.
2. Let thicken by setting mixture aside a few minutes.
3. Eat as is or this may also be added to ingredients when you make pancakes!

Belgian Waffle Mix with Cherry Sauce
Mix-in-a-Jar

These thick, hearty waffles are a family favorite and are very tasty served with cherry sauce and whipped cream topping.

Ingredients for cherry sauce:

¼	c. sugar
2	tsp. cornstarch
⅛	tsp. cinnamon
½	c. orange juice
2	c. sweet cherries
1	tsp. orange peel, grated

Ingredients for waffles:

2	c. flour
2	Tbs. sugar
1½	tsp. baking powder
½	tsp. salt

Directions for cherry sauce:

1. In saucepan, combine sugar, cornstarch, and cinnamon; add orange juice, cherries, and orange peel.
2. Bring to a boil over medium-high heat; boil until thickened.
3. Place cherry syrup in glass canning jar and seal.

Directions for waffles:

1. Combine flour, sugar, baking powder, and salt.
2. Put waffle mixture in glass canning jar.

Directions for Tag

Additional Ingredients:

1	jar Belgian Waffle Mix
2	c. milk
½	c. butter, melted
4	eggs yolks, beaten
4	egg whites, beaten stiff
	sweetened whipped cream

Directions:

1. In large bowl, combine milk, melted butter, and egg yolks.
2. Add waffle mix; stir just to moisten.
3. Fold in stiffly beaten egg whites.
4. Bake in waffle iron according to manufacturer's instructions.
5. Serve topped with Cherry Sauce and sweetened whipped cream.

Blueberry Pancake Mix-in-a-Jar

My family loves blueberries and this mix makes a delicious treat.

Ingredients:

1¼	c. flour
1	Tbs. baking powder
½	tsp. salt
¼	c. brown sugar
½	c. dried blueberries

Directions:

1. In medium bowl, combine flour, baking powder, and salt.
2. Pour into clean, dry 1-quart wide-mouth jar. A rolled piece of paper makes a perfect funnel for this.
3. Pack the layer down with a ladle.
4. Add brown sugar to jar and pack down.
5. Add dried blueberries and pack down.
6. Seal jar.

Directions for Tag

Additional Ingredients:

1	jar Blueberry Pancake Mix
1¼	c. milk
1	egg, beaten
2	Tbs. canola oil

Directions:

1. In large bowl, mix milk, egg, and oil.
2. Add pancake mix to wet ingredients and mix until just combined.
3. Heat skillet or frying pan to medium-high; give generous coating of cooking spray.
4. Drop batter in ¼ cup amounts to make pancakes.
5. Cook until edges dry and middles fill with bubbles.
6. Flip and cook other side until golden brown, about 2 or 3 minutes per side.
7. Serve with butter and maple syrup. Enjoy!

Yields: 4 servings.

Breakfast Fruit Chews Mix-in-a-Jar

These wholesome energy bars will be a welcome Christmas gift.

Ingredients:

1½	c. raisins
1	c. dried apricots
1	c. pitted dates
1	c. coconut, flaked
1	c. walnuts, finely chopped, divided

Directions:

1. In blender container, grind raisins, apricots, and dates.
2. In large bowl, combine ground fruit with coconut and ½ cup walnuts; mix well.
3. Shape mixture into thirty 1-inch balls.
4. Spread remaining ½ cup chopped nuts on a plate.
5. Roll balls in nuts, pressing nuts firmly into them.
6. No cooking! Place in wide-mouth glass canning jars and enjoy.

Directions for Tag

1. Transfer snack mix to serving bowl and enjoy. Or, eat it right out of the jar!

Buttermilk Pancake Mix-in-a-Jar

Buttermilk pancakes are another old-fashioned classic.

Ingredients:

2	c. buttermilk powder
8	c. all-purpose flour
½	c. sugar
8	tsp. baking powder
4	tsp. baking soda
2	tsp. salt

Directions:

1. In large bowl, sift ingredients together well. Pour into clean, dry 1-quart wide-mouth jar.
2. Seal and decorate, attach recipe tag.

Directions for Tag

Additional Ingredients:

1	jar Buttermilk Pancake Mix
1	egg, beaten
2	Tbs. canola oil
1	c. water or more if needed

Directions:

1. In medium bowl, combine egg, oil, and water; stir in pancake mix until blended. Let stand 5 minutes.
2. Lightly oil and preheat griddle. Pour about ⅓ cup batter for each pancake.
3. Cook until edge is dry and bubbles form.
4. Turn with wide spatula, cook 35 to 45 seconds longer until browned on both sides. Repeat with remaining batter.

Chocolate Chip Coffeecake Mix-in-a-Jar

Chocolate chips add moistness and flavor to this coffee cake mix.

Ingredients:

1½	c. all-purpose flour
¼	c. sugar
1	tsp. baking powder
1	tsp. baking soda
¼	tsp. salt
¾	c. brown sugar
1	c. chocolate chips
½	c. walnuts or pecans, chopped

Directions:

1. In medium bowl, sift flour, sugar, baking powder, baking soda, and salt.
2. Pour into clean, dry wide-mouth quart jar.
3. Layer the following ingredients on top of flour mix: brown sugar, chocolate chips, and chopped nuts.
4. Seal the jar.

Directions for Tag

Ingredients for Chocolate Chip Coffeecake:

1	jar Chocolate Chip Coffeecake Mix
3	eggs
½	c. butter, softened
1	tsp. vanilla extract
1	c. sour cream

Directions:

1. Preheat oven to 350 degrees F.
2. Prepare a 12 x 12-inch baking pan with a generous coating of cooking spray.
3. In large bowl, beat eggs, butter, and vanilla until well-blended.
4. Add coffee cake mix and sour cream mix until well- blended.
5. Pour batter into prepared pan.
6. Bake 25 to 35 minutes or until wooden toothpick inserted into center comes out clean.
7. Allow coffee cake to cool at least 10 minutes before cutting or consuming.

Yields: 12 servings.

Cinnamon and Brown Sugar Oatmeal
Mix-in-a-Jar

Need a simple gift that will make an easy breakfast for someone special? Then this is it!

Ingredients:

1	c. oatmeal
1	tsp. cinnamon
¼	c. brown sugar
1	c. oatmeal

Directions:

1. Use clean, dry 1-pint canning jar.
2. Layer ingredients in pint jar in order given.
3. Seal and decorate, attach recipe tag to jar.

Directions for Tag

Directions:

Microwave Method:

1. Add 2 cups water and microwave for 45 seconds.
2. Top with a splash of milk and enjoy!

Cinnamon Pancake Mix-in-a-Jar

You can personalize this gift by adding your favorite dried fruits. This will also add some welcome color and flavor to this Christmas gift.

Ingredients:

3	c. all-purpose flour
3	Tbs. sugar
2	Tbs. baking powder
4½	tsp. ground cinnamon
1¼	tsp. salt
	dried fruits, optional

Directions:

1. In large bowl, combine flour, sugar, baking powder, cinnamon, and salt.
2. Pour into 1-quart wide-mouth jar and pack firmly.
3. Place dried fruits into a sandwich bag and place on top of mix.
4. Seal and decorate, attach recipe tag to jar.

Directions for Tag

For 1 batch Cinnamon Pancakes, you will need:

1⅓	c. Cinnamon Pancake Mix
1	egg, slightly beaten
¾	c. milk
2	Tbs. canola oil

Directions:

1. In large bowl, combine egg, milk, and oil.
2. Pour in pancake mix and blend until just moistened.
3. Make pancakes as you normally would.

Cranberry Granola Mix-in-a-Jar

We usually have a bowl out during the holidays as pre-feast snack food. Enjoy!

Ingredients:

4	c. rolled oats
1	c. wheat germ
½	c. almonds, chopped
½	c. walnuts, chopped
1	c. dried cranberries
⅓	c. canola oil
1	c. honey
1½	tsp. vanilla extract
1	tsp. ground cinnamon

Directions:

1. Preheat oven to 300 degrees F.
2. In large bowl, stir together oats, wheat germ, nuts, and dried cranberries.
3. In medium saucepan, on medium heat, stir together oil, honey, vanilla, and cinnamon.
4. Heat until just warm and well combined.
5. Drizzle warm, wet mixture over dry ingredients; stir to coat evenly.
6. Spread mixture in a thin layer on an ungreased baking sheet.
7. Bake 30 to 40 minutes, stirring every 10 minutes to toast evenly.
8. Allow to cool completely before pouring into an airtight glass jar.
9. Granola will become crunchy as it cools.
10. Great as a snack or as a cereal with milk.

Yields: 10 servings.

1.   Transfer snack mix to serving bowl and enjoy. Or, eat it right
      out of the jar!

Gingerbread Pancake Mix-in-a-Jar

Homemade pancakes make a great weekend breakfast and a welcome Christmas gift. Enjoy!

Ingredients:

1	c. cake flour
1	c. all-purpose flour
½	c. buttermilk powder (or plain dry milk)
⅓	c. plus 1 Tbs. sugar
1	Tbs. baking powder
2	tsp. ground ginger
½	tsp. cinnamon
¼	tsp. salt
⅛	tsp. ground cloves
¾	c. white chocolate chips

Directions:

1. In large bowl, combine all ingredients except chocolate chips; mix thoroughly.
2. Pour 1 cup of the flour mixture into 1-quart wide-mouth jar.
3. Pack down layer with ladle.
4. Sprinkle chocolate chips into jar to create thin layer.
5. Continue adding flour mixture and chips alternately until all ingredients are used and your jar is full and very beautiful.
6. Seal jar.

Directions for Tag

Ingredients for Gingerbread Pancakes:

6	Tbs. butter, softened
2	eggs
1¾	c. water, divided

Directions:

1. In large bowl, beat eggs, butter, and ⅛ of water.
2. Alternately beat in pancake mix and remaining water.
3. Heat large frying pan or skillet on medium-high.
4. Grease surface with thin coat of cooking spray.
5. Drop batter in ¼ cup amounts per pancake.
6. Cook until bubbles appear on surface and edges are dry, about 2 or 3 minutes.
7. Flip and cook 2 to 3 minutes, or until golden brown.
8. Serve with butter and maple syrup. Enjoy!

Yields: 6 servings.

Gingersnap Granola Mix-in-a-Jar

Ginger, cinnamon, and nutmeg combine to make the perfect Christmas fragrance. Enjoy!

Ingredients:

3	Tbs. butter
½	c. honey
2	Tbs. molasses
2	tsp. lemon peel, grated
1	tsp. vanilla extract
½	tsp. ground ginger
¼	tsp. ground cinnamon
¼	tsp. salt
1	pinch grated nutmeg
2½	c. Oat Squares (or Oat Bran or Oat Chex cereal)
2	c. oats, quick or old-fashioned

Directions:

1. Preheat oven to 325 degrees F.
2. Prepare a 15 x 10-inch rimmed baking sheet by spraying with a thin coating of cooking spray.
3. In small saucepan, on medium-low heat, combine butter, honey, molasses, lemon peel, vanilla, and remaining spices. Cook, stirring often until well combined and smooth.
4. In large bowl, mix breakfast cereal and uncooked oats together.
5. Drizzle with hot mixture and stir gently to coat evenly.
6. Spread combined mixture on prepared baking sheet.
7. Bake 25 to 30 minutes, or until golden brown, stirring every 10 minutes.
8. Begin checking granola after 20 minutes so it doesn't burn.
9. Place completely cooled granola into glass canning jar and seal.
10. Good for about 2 weeks.

Yields: 8 servings.

Directions for Tag

1. Transfer snack mix to serving bowl and enjoy. Or, eat it right out of the jar!

Granola Mix-in-a-Jar

This mix is simple and can be tailored to your own taste. Great gift for breakfast or snacks.

Ingredients:

2	lb. rolled oats
1	c. nuts, chopped (your favorite kind)
¾	c. sunflower seeds
1	c. wheat germ
2	tsp. salt
1½	c. canola oil
¼	c. water
3	Tbs. vanilla extract
1½	c. honey

Directions:

1. Preheat oven to 200 degrees F.
2. Well grease a large baking sheet.
3. In large mixing bowl, combine first 5 ingredients.
4. In medium bowl, combine last 4 ingredients.
5. Combine and mix contents of both bowls.
6. Spread mixture onto prepared baking sheet.
7. Bake 1½ hour, stirring occasionally.
8. Stores well for weeks in glass canning jar.

Yields: 16 servings

Directions for Tag

1. Transfer snack mix to serving bowl and enjoy. Or, eat it right out of the jar!

Granola Mix-in-a-Jar

This makes a tasty breakfast cereal. It is also great as a snack or in a lunch.

Ingredients:

5½	c. rolled oats
2½	c. coconut, unsweetened
1	c. almonds, slivered
½	c. sesame seeds
1½	tsp. salt
4	tsp. cinnamon
2	Tbs. vanilla extract
¾	c. canola oil
⅓	c. molasses
1	c. honey
¾	c. pecan pcs.
¾	c. hazelnuts

Directions:

1. Preheat oven to 400 degrees F.
2. Lightly grease baking sheets.
3. In large bowl, combine dry ingredients.
4. In medium saucepan, add all wet ingredients; simmer but do not boil.
5. Pour hot, wet ingredients over dry; stir to combine.
6. Put a thin layer of granola on prepared sheets to bake.
7. Bake 30 to 45 minutes, stirring often.
8. Place cooled granola in gift jars and seal.

Directions for Tag

1. Transfer snack mix to serving bowl and enjoy. Or, eat it right out of the jar!

Raisin and Brown Sugar Instant Oatmeal Mix-in-a-Jar

Ready for a quick breakfast treat? This makes a welcome meal for a simple yet delicious breakfast.

Ingredients:

3	c. quick-cooking oatmeal
⅓	c. brown sugar
2	Tbs. dry milk powder
1	tsp. cinnamon
¾	tsp. salt
¾	c. raisins

Directions:

1. In large bowl, combine all ingredients except raisins; mix thoroughly.
2. Pour 1 cup oat mixture into 1-quart jar.
3. Pack down layer with a ladle.
4. Sprinkle raisins into jar to create a thin layer.
5. Continue adding oats and raisins alternately until all ingredients are used, and your jar is full and very pretty.
6. Seal jar.

Directions for Tag

Ingredients for Raisin and Brown Sugar Oatmeal Mix:

1c.	Raisin and Brown Sugar Oatmeal Mix
1½	c. water

Directions:

Boiling Water Method:

1. Pour boiling water over oatmeal mix and stir.
2. Let stand a couple of minutes until thickened to desired consistency.

Microwave Method:

1. In large microwavable cereal bowl, stir oatmeal mix and water together.
2. Microwave for 1½ minutes.
3. Stir and microwave 1 minute more.
4. Let stand for 1 minute before serving.
5. Top with a splash of milk and enjoy!

Yields: 2 servings.

Whole Grain Lentil Breakfast
Cereal Mix-in-a-Jar

This cereal is very delicious and is a nutritious and healthy way to start your busy day.

Ingredients

¼	c. whole wheat berries
¼	c. whole rye berries
¼	c. whole triticale
¼	c. whole barley
¼	c. brown rice
¼	c. buckwheat groats
¼	c. millet
¼	c. sesame seeds
¼	c. flaxseed
¼	c. lentils
2½	c. oat groats /or/ oatmeal (old-fashioned)

Directions:

1. Mix all ingredients and place in glass canning jars.

Directions for Tag

1. In large saucepan, measure 2 cups Whole Grain Lentil Breakfast Cereal Mix to 5 cups water.
2. Bring to boil; let sit overnight.
3. Heat 1 bowlful each morning in microwave until cooked cereal is gone.
4. For one serving, heat ¼ cup of cereal to ¾ cup water. It's very chewy and satisfying.

Whole Wheat Waffle
Mix-in-a-Jar

Waffles are a welcome breakfast treat and this gift makes morning breakfast a lot easier.

Ingredients:

- ¾ c. whole wheat flour
- ¾ c. all-purpose flour
- 2 Tbs. sugar
- 2 tsp. baking powder
- ¾ tsp. salt

Directions:

1. In medium bowl, combine all ingredients.
2. Pour mixture into 1-pint wide-mouth jar. A rolled piece of paper makes a great funnel.
3. Seal jar.

Directions for Tag

Additional Ingredients:

- 1 jar Whole Wheat Waffle Mix
- 1 c. milk
- 4 Tbs. canola oil
- 2 eggs, beaten

Directions:

1. In large bowl, mix all ingredients together.
2. Cook on a lightly-greased preheated waffle iron according to manufacturer's instructions.

Yields: 4 servings.

Christmas Gifts-in-a-Jar Cookbook
A Collection of Christmas Gifts-in-a-Jar Recipes
Gifts-in-a-Jar Cookbook Series – Book 1

Cakes

Table of Contents

Applesauce Cake-in-a-Jar

Applesauce cake is an old-fashioned favorite. This makes a welcome gift for the holidays.

Ingredients:

2⅔	c. shortening
2⅔	c. sugar
4	eggs
2	c. applesauce
⅓	c. water
3⅓	c. all-purpose flour, sifted
½	tsp. baking powder
2	tsp. baking soda
1½	tsp. salt
1	tsp. cinnamon
2	tsp. cloves
⅔	c. walnuts, chopped

Directions:

1. Preheat oven to 325 degrees F.
2. In large bowl, cream together shortening and sugar.
3. Beat in eggs, one at a time, until mixture is light and fluffy.
4. Add applesauce and water; set aside.
5. In medium bowl, sift together flour, baking powder, baking soda, salt, cinnamon, and cloves.
6. Blend dry ingredients into applesauce mixture. Fold in nuts.
7. Sterilize pint (wide-mouth jam/jelly) jars, lids, and rings. Keep lids and rings in hot water until ready to use.
8. Grease insides of jars with shortening. Do not use Pam. Fill jars half full.
9. Place jars on baking sheet.

10. Bake 45 minutes or until wooden toothpick inserted in center of each cake comes out clean.
11. Remove jars from oven one at a time, wipe rim of jar clean; put on lid and ring. Screw on tightly.
12. Jars will seal as cakes cool.

Butterscotch Brownie Mix-in-a-Jar

Everyone loves chocolate brownies and this makes a welcome change of flavor for this popular treat.

Ingredients:

2	c. all-purpose flour
1½	Tbs. baking powder
¼	tsp. salt
½	c. coconut, flaked
¾	c. pecans, chopped
2	c. brown sugar, firmly packed

Directions:

1. In medium bowl, combine flour, baking powder, and salt.
2. Layer ingredients in order given in 1-quart wide-mouth canning jar.
3. Press each layer firmly in place before adding next ingredient.

Directions for Tag

Ingredients:

1	jar Butterscotch Brownie Mix
¾	c. butter, softened
2	eggs, slightly beaten
2	tsp. vanilla extract

Directions:

1. Preheat oven to 375 degrees F.
2. Lightly grease a 9 x 13-inch metal baking pan.
3. In large bowl, empty Butterscotch Brownie Mix. Use your hands to thoroughly blend mix.
4. Add butter, eggs, and vanilla; mix until completely blended.
5. Spread batter into prepared baking pan.

6. Bake 25 minutes.
7. Let cool 15 minutes, cut into 1½-inch squares.

Yields: 2 dozen brownies.

Caramel Nut Cake-in-a-Jar

The texture of delicious walnuts adds flavor to this caramel goodness. Enjoy!

Ingredients:

3½	c. all-purpose flour
1	tsp. baking powder
2	tsp. baking soda
1	tsp. salt
2	c. brown sugar, packed
⅔	c. white sugar
1	c. butter, softened
4	eggs
⅔	c. milk
1	Tbs. vanilla extract
1	c. walnuts, chopped

Directions:

1. Preheat oven to 325 degrees F.
2. Sterilize 6 1-pint wide-mouth canning jars, lids, and rings by boiling 10 minutes.
3. Keep lids and rings in hot water until needed.
4. Dry jars and let them come to room temperature.
5. Grease insides of jars well.
6. In medium bowl, sift together flour, baking powder, soda, and salt. Set aside.
7. In large bowl, cream sugars and butter with electric mixer.
8. Add eggs and mix well.
9. Add milk and vanilla, mix well.
10. Add flour mixture and blend with large spoon.
11. Gently fold in nuts.
12. Place 1 cup batter into each greased canning jar.
13. Wipe any batter from rim.
14. Place jars on baking sheet. Bake 50 minutes or until wooden toothpick inserted deep into center of cake comes out clean.

15. Make sure jar rims are clean. If they're not, jars will not seal correctly.
16. While jars are still hot, place lids on jars, and screw rings on tightly.
17. Jars will seal as they cool. Place jars on counter and listen for them to "ping" as they seal.
18. If you miss the "ping", wait until they are completely cool and press on top of lid. If it doesn't move at all, it's sealed.

Carrot Cake Mix-in-a-Jar

Moist carrots and crunchy pecans make a tasty Christmas gift.

Ingredients:

2	c. sugar
2	tsp. vanilla, powdered
½	c. pecans, chopped
3	c. all-purpose flour
2	tsp. baking soda
1	Tbs. cinnamon
¼	tsp. nutmeg

Directions:

1. In small bowl, combine and blend ingredients.
2. Store in airtight jar.

Directions for Tag

Ingredients:

1	jar Carrot Cake Mix
1½	c. canola oil
3	eggs
3	c. carrots, grated
1	can pineapple, crushed (8 oz.)

Directions:

1. Preheat oven to 350 degrees F.
2. Grease 9 x 13-inch baking pan.
3. In large bowl, place carrot cake mix.
4. Make well in center of mix; add oil, eggs, carrots, and pineapple; blend until smooth.
5. Pour into prepared pan.
6. Bake 40 to 50 minutes or until wooden toothpick inserted into center comes out clean.
7. Cool cake and frost if desired or dust with powdered sugar.

Chewy Brownie Mix-in-a-Jar

This gift of brownie mix makes a popular favorite for Christmas gift giving.

Ingredients:

- 1⅔ c. sugar
- ¾ c. cocoa
- 1⅓ c. all-purpose flour
- ½ tsp. baking powder
- ¼ tsp. salt
- ¾ c. nuts, chopped

Directions:

1. Layer ingredients in order listed above in 1-quart wide-mouth jar, pressing firmly after adding each ingredient.

Directions for Tag

Ingredients:

- 1 jar of Chewy Brownie Mix
- ¾ c. butter, melted
- 2 eggs
- 2 Tbs. water
- 2 tsp. vanilla extract

Directions:

1. Preheat oven to 350 degrees F.
2. Lightly grease a 9 x 13-inch baking pan.
3. In large bowl, pour jar contents; stir.
4. Add butter, eggs, water, and vanilla; stir well.
5. Spread into prepared baking pan.
6. Bake 18 to 25 minutes or until wooden toothpick inserted in center comes out slightly sticky.
7. Cool in pan on wire rack.

Yields: 2 dozen brownies.

Chocolate Cake Mix-in-a-Jar

Chocolate is a familiar favorite and this makes a moist cake mix gift-in-a-jar.

Ingredients:

3	c. all-purpose flour
2	c. sugar
1	c. chocolate, ground
2	tsp. baking soda

Directions:

1. In large bowl, combine all ingredients and store in airtight jar.

Yields: 8 to 10 servings.

Directions for Tag

Ingredients for cake:

1	jar Chocolate Cake Mix
1	c. canola oil
1	c. buttermilk
2	eggs
1	c. boiling water
1	tsp. vanilla extract

Ingredients for cream cheese frosting:

1	lb. powdered sugar
1	pkg. cream cheese (3 oz.)
½	c. butter, softened
2	Tbs. milk
1	tsp. vanilla extract

Directions for cake:

1. Preheat oven to 350 degrees F.
2. Lightly grease a 9 x 13-inch baking pan.
3. In large bowl, place cake mix and add oil, buttermilk, eggs, water, and vanilla.
4. Mix on low speed for 3 minutes until mixture is smooth.
5. Pour batter into prepared pan.
6. Bake 30 to 40 minutes.
7. Remove from oven and let cake cool.

Directions for cream cheese frosting:

1. In small bowl, with electric mixer, cream together sugar, cream cheese, and butter.
2. Gradually add milk and vanilla, and beat mixture until it is smooth.
3. Frost cooled cake.

Chocolate Truffle Pound Cake
Mix-in-a-Jar

Moist pound cake provides a welcome treat for Christmas.

Ingredients:

3	c. sugar
3	c. all-purpose flour
½	tsp. salt
1	tsp. baking soda
½	c. cocoa

Directions:

1. Combine ingredients and pour in airtight jar.

Directions for Tag

Ingredients:

1	jar Chocolate Truffle Pound Cake Mix
¾	c. butter
5	eggs
1	c. milk
1	tsp. vanilla extract

Directions:

1. Preheat oven to 325 degrees F.
2. Butter a 9-cup Bundt pan.
3. In large bowl of electric mixer, cream butter until smooth.
4. Add eggs one at a time, beating after each.
5. Add milk and vanilla, beating mixture until thoroughly blended.
6. Add mix and continue to beat for 3 minutes until smooth.
7. Pour into prepared pan.

8. Bake 1 hour and 5 minutes or until wooden toothpick inserted into middle comes out clean.
9. Cool 25 minutes in pan.
10. Remove from pan and cool on wire rack.

Crazy Cake Mix-in-a-Jar

This is a simple moist Christmas gift-in-a-jar. Enjoy!

Ingredients:

2	c. all-purpose flour
⅔	c. cocoa powder
¾	tsp. salt
1½	tsp. baking powder
1⅓	c. sugar

Directions:

1. Layer ingredients in a 1-quart canning jar. It is helpful to tap jar lightly on a padded surface (towel on counter) as you layer ingredients to make all ingredients fit neatly.
2. Use scissors to cut a 9-inch diameter circle fabric of your choice.
3. Center fabric circle over lid and secure with rubber band.
4. Tie on raffia or ribbon bow to cover rubber band. Attach card with following directions.

Directions for Tag

Ingredients:

¾	c. canola oil
2	tsp. vinegar
1	tsp. vanilla extract
2	c. water

Directions:

1. Preheat oven to 350 degrees F.
2. In large bowl, stir cake ingredients together using a wire whisk or fork, making certain all ingredients are completely mixed together.

3. Bake 35 minutes or until wooden toothpick inserted into middle comes out clean.
4. Frost as desired or serve sprinkled with powdered sugar, with fresh fruit on side.

Gingerbread Mix-in-a-Jar

Fragrant and delicious gingerbread makes a welcome Christmas gift. Enjoy!

Ingredients:

2¼	c. all-purpose flour
¾	c. sugar
1	tsp. baking soda
½	tsp. baking powder
¼	tsp. salt
2	tsp. ginger
1	tsp. cinnamon
½	tsp. cloves
¾	c. butter, softened
¾	c. water
½	c. molasses

Directions:

1. Preheat oven to 325 degrees F.
2. Place baking sheet onto middle rack.
3. Before starting batter, wash 5 12-ounce jars, lids, and rings in hot soapy water and let drain, dry, and cool to room temperature.
4. Generously prepare inside of jars with butter.
5. In large bowl, combine flour, sugar, baking soda, baking powder, salt, ginger, cinnamon, and cloves.
6. In medium bowl, combine butter, water, and molasses. Mix with dry ingredients.
7. Divide batter among jars; should be slightly less than half full.
8. Carefully wipe rims clean, place jars on baking sheet (or they'll tip over) in center of oven.
9. Bake 40 minutes.
10. Keep lids in hot water until they're used.
11. When cakes are done, remove jars, which are hot, from oven one at a time.

12. If rims need cleaning, use moistened paper towel.
13. Carefully put lids and rings in place, screw tops on tightly shut.
14. Place jars on wire rack; they will seal as they cool.

Yields: 5 12-ounce jars.

Lemon Poppy-Seed Cake Mix-in-a-Jar

Poppy seed is a family favorite and the lemon addition makes it a tasty Christmas gift.

Ingredients:

1½	c. sugar
3	c. cake flour
1½	tsp. baking powder
¼	c. poppy seeds

Directions for cake mix:

1. In large bowl, blend all ingredients together except poppy seeds.
2. Pour into airtight jar.
3. Place poppy seeds into baggie and place bag inside jar or attach baggie to outside.

Directions for Tag

Ingredients for cake:

1	jar Lemon Poppy Seed Cake Mix
¾	c. butter
6	eggs
⅓	c. milk
1	tsp. vanilla extract
1	tsp. lemon extract
1	lemon, zest

Ingredients for glaze:

½	c. sugar
½	c. lemon juice

Directions for cake:

1. Preheat oven to 350 degrees F.
2. Butter 8 to 9-cup Bundt pan.
3. In large bowl, with electric mixer, cream butter.
4. Add eggs, one at a time, beating after each.
5. Add milk, extracts, and zest. Mixture will look curdled.
6. Add mix and continue to beat on medium speed for 3 to 4 minutes until mixture is smooth.
7. Stir in poppy seeds.
8. Pour batter into prepared pan.
9. Bake 45 to 55 minutes. While cake is baking, make glaze.

Directions for glaze:

1. In small saucepan, over medium heat, combine sugar and lemon juice; bring mixture to boil for 3 minutes.
2. When cake has been removed from oven, poke cake all over with a wooden skewer, and brush glaze over cake.
3. Let cake stand for 1 hour; remove from pan to cool on a wire rack.
4. Wrap cake when it is cooled.

Yields: 8 servings.

Mocha Brownie Mix-in-a-Jar

Mocha adds wonderful flavor to these delicious brownies.

Ingredients:

2¼	c. sugar
¼	c. powdered milk
⅔	c. cocoa powder, unsweetened
1	tsp. instant coffee
1¼	c. all-purpose flour
1	tsp. baking powder
1	tsp. salt

Directions:

1. Use clean, dry 1-quart wide-mouth jar and press each layer down firmly.
2. Pour in sugar and powdered milk.
3. Follow with cocoa powder and coffee.
4. Combine flour, baking powder, and salt; layer them last.

Directions for Tag

Ingredients:

¾	c. butter, softened
4	eggs, slightly beaten

Directions:

1. Preheat oven to 350 degrees F.
2. Lightly grease 9 x 13-inch baking pan.
3. In large bowl, empty Cappuccino Brownie Mix; mix thoroughly.
4. Add butter and eggs; mix until completely blended.
5. Spread batter into prepared pan.

6. Bake 30 minutes or until wooden toothpick inserted into middle comes out clean.
7. Cool in pan. Cut into 2-inch squares.

Yields: 2 dozen brownies.

Pina Colada Cake Mix-in-a-Jar

Moist pineapple, rum, and coconut combined to make a delicious flavor. Yum!

Ingredients:

1	can pineapple, unsweetened crushed (20 oz.)
1	stick plus 3 Tbs. unsalted butter, softened (11 Tbs.)
3½	c. light brown sugar, divided
4	eggs
½	c. dark rum
3⅓	c. flour
1½	tsp. baking powder
1	tsp. baking soda
1	c. coconut, sweetened flaked

Directions:

1. Preheat oven to 325 degrees F.
2. Before starting batter, wash 8 1-pint wide-mouth canning jars with lids in hot, soapy water and let them drain, dry, and cool to room temperature.
3. Generously grease inside of jars.
4. Drain crushed pineapple for about 10 minutes in a colander, reserving juice.
5. Purée drained pineapple in a food processor.
6. Measure out 1½ cups purée, adding a little juice if necessary to make 1½ cups. Set purée aside.
7. Discard remaining juice or reserve for another use.
8. In large bowl, with electric mixer, beat together butter and half of brown sugar until light and fluffy.
9. Beat in eggs and remaining sugar.
10. Beat in pineapple purée and rum; set aside.
11. In another bowl, sift flour, baking powder, and baking soda together.
12. Gradually add to pineapple mixture in thirds, beating well after each addition to make thick batter.

13. Stir in coconut.
14. Spoon 1 level cupful of batter into each jar.
15. Carefully wipe rims clean, place jars in center of preheated oven. Bake 40 minutes.
16. In medium saucepan, about 10 minutes before cakes are done, bring water to a boil. Put in jar lids, cover, and remove from heat.
17. Keep lids in hot water until they're used.
18. When cakes are done, remove jars from oven.
19. If jar rims need cleaned, use a moistened paper towel.
20. Carefully put lids and rings in place, screw tops tightly shut.
21. Place jars on wire rack; they will seal as they cool.

Yields: 8 cakes.

Pumpkin Spice Cake Mix-in-a-Jar

Pumpkin cake is always appreciated in our house. Everyone will enjoy this moist Christmas treat.

Ingredients:

1	c. raisins
1	c. walnuts
2	c. flour
2	tsp. baking soda
¼	tsp. baking powder
½	tsp. salt
2	tsp. ground cloves
2	tsp. cinnamon
1	tsp. ground ginger
4	eggs
2	c. sugar
1	c. canola oil
1	can pumpkin (15 oz.)

Directions:

1. Preheat oven to 325 degrees F.
2. Wash 8 1-pint jars, lids, and rings in hot, soapy water; rinse well.
3. Allow jars to air dry. Once jars are dry, generously grease inside of each jar with shortening.
4. Coarsely chop raisins and walnuts; set aside.
5. In large bowl, sift together dry ingredients.
6. Add raisins and walnuts; toss to lightly combine.
7. In medium bowl, beat eggs at high speed until thick and lemon colored, about 3 minutes.
8. Gradually beat in sugar until thick and light.
9. At low speed, beat in oil and pumpkin; blend well.
10. Gradually stir in flour mixture until well blended.
11. Divide batter among jars, they should be slightly less than half full.

12. Wipe any batter from rim of jars.
13. Place jars on baking sheet; bake 35 to 40 minutes or until wooden toothpick inserted into center of each jar comes out clean.
14. While cakes are baking, place lids and rings in pan of water and bring to a boil.
15. Remove from heat, and leave them in water until cakes are done.
16. Remove cakes from oven one at a time, place lids and rings on them and tighten.
17. Allow jars to cool, check to be sure they have sealed.
18. There should be no movement on lid.
19. If any have not sealed, eat them within a week.

Yields: 8 1-pint jars.

White Chocolate Brownie Mix-in-a-Jar

White chocolate brownies make a nice diversity from the traditional chocolate brownie. Enjoy!

Ingredients:

¾	c. all-purpose flour
½	tsp. salt
½	tsp. baking powder
½	c. cocoa, unsweetened
1	c. white chocolate chips or chunks
¾	c. walnuts or pecans, chopped
1	c. sugar

Directions:

1. In 1-quart wide-mouth canning jar, layer flour, salt, and baking powder, using canning funnel.
2. Add cocoa; shake jar just slightly to level layer.
3. Add white chocolate chips, walnuts, or pecans.
4. Put sugar in small food storage bag; seal or tie well, then shape into small enough shape to fit into top of jar.
5. Press sugar bag into top of jar.

Directions for Tag

Ingredients:

1	jar White Chocolate Brownie Mix
4	oz. butter, softened
2	eggs
1	tsp. vanilla extract

Directions:

1. Preheat oven to 350 degrees F.
2. Grease and flour an 8-inch baking pan.
3. Take bag of sugar from top of canning jar and pour into mixing bowl.
4. Add softened butter; beat until light in color.
5. Beat in eggs and vanilla until creamy.
6. Empty remainder of jar into mixing bowl.
7. Stir with wooden spoon until dry ingredients are well moistened. Mixture will be stiff.
8. Spread brownie batter into prepared pan.
9. Bake 20 to 25 minutes, or until brownies are set.
10. Cool in pan before cutting into squares.

Christmas Gifts-in-a-Jar Cookbook
A Collection of Christmas Gifts-in-a-Jar Recipes
Gifts-in-a-Jar Cookbook Series – Book 1

Candies

Table of Contents

Brandy Balls-in-a-Jar

This is a delicious hit at holiday gatherings. Make them a day ahead.

1   can evaporated milk (5 oz.)
1   c. semisweet chocolate chips
½   c. brandy
1   pkg. vanilla wafers, crushed very fine (16 oz.)
2   c. walnuts, finely chopped
1   c. powdered sugar, for rolling

Directions:

1. In microwave or metal bowl, over a pan of simmering water, add evaporated milk and chocolate chips, stirring frequently until smooth.
2. Remove from heat; stir in brandy and crushed vanilla wafers until well blended.
3. Roll dough into small balls, roll in chopped walnuts, then powdered sugar.
4. Place into wide-mouth jars and seal with lids.
5. Store in refrigerator.

Yields: 5 dozen.

Candy Cane Bark-in-a-Jar

Candy canes are a traditional Christmas treat and make a welcome gift.

Ingredients:

1¼   c. candy canes, crushed, divided (22-28 standard size)
2   bags white candy bark morsels (12 oz.)

Directions:

1. Unwrap candy canes and place in Ziploc bag.
2. Crush candy canes with rolling pin, until you have them your desired texture.
3. In large microwave-safe bowl, place chips; microwave for 45 seconds, stir. Microwave in increments of 30 seconds, until morsels are melted.
4. Stir in half of crushed candy canes to melted morsels, spread out evenly on foil-lined baking sheet.
5. Sprinkle remaining half of crushed candy pieces.
6. Place in refrigerator 1 hour to let harden.
7. Break into pieces.
8. Place in jars and seal with lids.

Caramel Popcorn Mix-in-a-Jar

This caramel corn never lasts very long - it is so good!

Ingredients:

1	c. sugar
1	c. brown sugar, packed
1⅓	c. popcorn, unpopped
	dash of salt

Directions:

1. Layer sugars in a 1-quart canning jar.
2. Place popcorn into small zip baggie; seal baggie and place on top of sugars.
3. Place lid on jar.

Directions for Tag

Ingredients:

1	jar Caramel Popcorn Mix
1	can sweetened condensed milk (14 oz.)

Directions:

1. Preheat oven to 300 degrees F.
2. Pop popcorn and remove all unpopped kernels.
3. Place popcorn in roasting pan; keep warm in oven.
4. In medium saucepan, combine milk, sugars, and salt.
5. Heat and stir over medium heat 4 to 5 minutes.
6. Pour milk mixture over popcorn; stir gently to coat.
7. Bake 20 minutes, stirring every 5 minutes.
8. Allow to cool in pan, break into pieces or clusters.

Chocolate Covered Caramels-in-a-Jar

These caramels are wonderful, with or without the chocolate coating!

Ingredients:

1	c. butter
2¼	c. brown sugar
1	c. light corn syrup
1	can sweetened condensed milk (14 oz.)
1	tsp. vanilla extract
1	lb. milk chocolate
1	Tbs. butter

Directions

1. Grease an 8 x 8-inch square pan.
2. In heavy 4-quart saucepan, melt butter over medium heat; add brown sugar, corn syrup, and milk.
3. Stirring constantly, heat to 242 to 248 degrees F. until small amount of syrup dropped into cold water forms firm but pliable ball.
4. Remove from heat and stir in vanilla.
5. Pour into prepared pan.
6. When caramel has cooled and set, cut into 1-inch squares; chill in refrigerator until firm.
7. Melt chocolate with butter in top of double boiler or bowl in microwave.
8. Stir until smooth.
9. Dip caramel squares in chocolate and place on wax paper to cool.
10. Place into wide-mouth jars and seal with lids.

Yields: 120 pieces.

Chocolate Covered
Orange Balls-in-a-Jar

This is a refreshing holiday treat and a delicious break from the "norm" with the orange blended with chocolate and walnuts!

Ingredients:

1	lb. powdered sugar
1	pkg. vanilla wafers, crushed (12 oz.)
1	c. walnuts, chopped
¼	lb. butter
1	can frozen orange juice concentrate, thawed (6 oz.)
1½	lb. milk chocolate, melted

Directions:

1. In large bowl, mix sugar, vanilla wafers, walnuts, butter, and orange juice.
2. Shape into 1-inch round balls; allow to dry for 1 hour.
3. Place chocolate in top of double boiler.
4. Stir frequently over medium heat until melted.
5. Dip balls into melted chocolate and place in decorative paper cups.
6. Place into glass wide-mouth jar and seal with lid.

Yields: 3 dozen.

Chocolate Covered Peppermint Patties-in-a-Jar

These peppermint patties are made with mashed potatoes and are the favorite of many of our friends!

Ingredients:

1	c. potatoes, mashed
1	tsp. salt
2	Tbs. butter, melted
2	tsp. peppermint extract
8	c. powdered sugar
8	squares semisweet chocolate (1 oz.)
2	Tbs. shortening

Directions:

1. In large bowl, mix together potatoes, salt, butter, and peppermint extract.
2. Gradually mix in powdered sugar; mix in enough to make workable dough, between 6 and 8 cups.
3. Knead slightly, roll into cherry-size balls.
4. Flatten balls to form patties; arrange on sheets of wax paper, allow to dry overnight.
5. In microwave-safe bowl, heat chocolate and shortening, stirring occasionally until melted and smooth.
6. Dip patties in melted chocolate, let cool on wax paper.
7. Place cooled patties in glass wide-mouth jars and seal with lids.

Yields: 4 dozen.

Chocolate Peanut Butter Bars-in-a-Jar

You will love these peanut butter bars. They just melt in your mouth!

Ingredients:

3	c. sugar
1	c. light corn syrup
½	c. water
1	jar creamy peanut butter, melted (18 oz.)
1½	lb. milk chocolate

Directions:

1. Butter a baking sheet well.
2. In large heavy saucepan, combine sugar, corn syrup, and water.
3. Cook and stir over low heat until sugar is dissolved; bring to full rolling boil.
4. Boil, stirring constantly to soft-crack stage at 290 degrees F.
5. In large greased heatproof bowl, place melted peanut butter.
6. Pour hot syrup over peanut butter; stir quickly until blended and pour onto prepared baking sheet.
7. Cover with piece of buttered waxed paper. Roll out mixture into 14 x 12-inch rectangle; remove waxed paper.
8. While warm, cut 1½ x 1-inch bars using buttered pizza cutter or knife. Cool completely.
9. Melt chocolate, dip bars, and place on waxed paper to harden.
10. Place in glass wide-mouth jars and seal with lid.

Yields: 72 servings

Chocolate Raspberry Bonbons-in-a-Jar

This is a favorite for every chocolate-lover. Enjoy!

Ingredients:

1	c. vanilla wafers, finely crushed
1	c. powdered sugar
1	c. almonds, chopped, toasted
2	Tbs. cocoa, unsweetened
2	Tbs. butter
¼	c. raspberry preserves, seedless
¼	c. raspberry liqueur
6	oz. sweet baking chocolate, grated

Directions for toasting almonds:

1. Spread almonds in single layer in heavy-bottomed skillet.
2. Cook over medium heat 1 to 2 minutes, stirring frequently, until almonds are lightly browned.
3. Remove from skillet immediately.
4. Cool before using.

Directions:

1. In large bowl, combine wafer crumbs, sugar, almonds, and cocoa.
2. In small microwave-safe bowl, heat butter and raspberry preserves until butter melts.
3. Blend butter mixture into crumb mixture; add raspberry liqueur.
4. Chill 1 hour, shape into 1-inch balls.
5. Roll balls in grated chocolate.
6. Place candy into glass jars and seal with lids.
7. May be stored in airtight container for up to 2 weeks.

Divinity-in-a-Jar

Divinity is always a "must have" on the holiday sweets tray. This is delicious.

Ingredients:

2½	c. sugar
½	c. light corn syrup
¼	tsp. salt
½	c. water
2	egg whites
1	tsp. vanilla extract

Directions:

1. In 2-quart saucepan, combine sugar, corn syrup, salt, and water.
2. Cook to hard-ball stage (260 degrees F.) stirring only until sugar dissolves.
3. In medium bowl, beat egg whites to stiff peaks.
4. Gradually pour syrup over egg whites, beating at high speed on electric mixer.
5. Add vanilla and beat until candy holds its shape, 4 to 5 minutes.
6. Quickly drop from teaspoon onto wax paper; cool.
7. Place in wide-mouth jar and seal with lid.

Yields: 4 servings.

Famous Caramel Cookie Bars-in-a-Jar

This combination of shortbread, caramel, and chocolate is truly a wonderful treat! I have such wonderful memories of the times I've enjoyed making these with my children's help.

Ingredients:

40	rectangular shortbread cookies
35	individually wrapped caramels, unwrapped
¼	c. water
4	c. milk chocolate chips

Directions:

1. Place shortbread cookies on baking sheet or tray.
2. In small saucepan, over medium-low heat, melt caramels in water, stirring frequently.
3. Spoon thin line of caramel over each cookie. Place cookies in refrigerator until caramel is set.
4. Line baking sheets or trays with waxed paper. In double boiler over simmering water, melt chocolate.
5. Dip cookies in chocolate one at a time, tapping against side of bowl to remove excess.
6. Place on prepared sheets and let rest at room temperature several hours, until set.
7. To speed up process after dipping, refrigerate for 30 minutes.
8. Place pieces in glass wide-mouth canning jar and seal.

Yields: 40 bars

Marshmallows-in-a-Jar

You know how great marshmallows are to top off your hot chocolate. Just like anything else homemade, the "store-purchased" version doesn't even start to compare with the homemade version. What a treat!

Ingredients:

1½	c. sugar
1	c. light corn syrup
1	c. water
8	egg whites
3	pkgs. unflavored gelatin, (1 oz. ea.)
1	Tbs. vanilla extract
3	c. powdered sugar, divided

Directions:

1. Line 8-inch-square cake pan with wax paper.
2. Generously coat with 1 cup powdered sugar; set aside.
3. In medium saucepan, combine sugar, corn syrup, and water.
4. Heat over medium heat 10 to 15 minutes, or until temperature on candy thermometer reaches (260 degrees F.) or hard-ball stage.
5. In medium bowl, whip egg whites until they form stiff peaks.
6. Add gelatin to syrup. Mix for 2 minutes, until lumps have disappeared.
7. While mixing at medium speed, slowly add thickened syrup to whipped egg whites.
8. When incorporated, add vanilla.
9. Continue to mix for 5 minutes, or until mixture feels lukewarm to touch.
10. Pour mixture into prepared pan. Smooth surface with spatula. Cool at room temperature.
11. To harden marshmallows, cover surface with additional 1 cup powdered sugar.
12. Top with wax paper.
13. Freeze for at least 1 hour or overnight.

14. Run knife under hot water.
15. Dust cutting board powdered with remaining 1 cup powdered sugar.
16. Cut marshmallows into squares on cutting board.
17. Store in canning jars in refrigerator.

Yields: 30 marshmallows.

Microwave Peanut Brittle-in-a-Jar

This peanut brittle is so easy to make, and so delicious!

Ingredients:

1	c. light corn syrup
2	c. sugar
⅔	c. peanuts
2	Tbs. butter
2	tsp. vanilla extract
2	tsp. baking soda

Directions:

1. Lightly butter a baking sheet.
2. In 3-quart casserole dish, combine corn syrup, sugar, and peanuts.
3. Microwave on high 12 minutes.
4. Stir in butter and vanilla; cook on high 4 minutes.
5. Stir in baking soda and pour onto prepared baking sheet.
6. Cool and break into pieces.
7. Place into wide-mouth jars and seal with lids.

Yields: 32 servings.

Peanut Butter Oatmeal Drops-in-a-Jar

These are just wonderful with the blend of peanut butter, oatmeal, nuts, and chocolate!

Ingredients:

½	c. butter
2	c. sugar
½	c. milk
2	tsp. cocoa
½	c. peanut butter
3	c. oatmeal, not instant
½	c. nuts, chopped, optional

Directions:

1. In large saucepan, mix butter, sugar, milk, and cocoa together.
2. Boil 1 minute, stirring constantly.
3. Remove from heat; stir in remaining ingredients.
4. Drop by teaspoonful onto wax paper and let harden.
5. Candy will set up in 30 to 60 minutes.
6. Note: These will keep for several days without refrigerating, up to 2 weeks refrigerated, and 2 to 3 months frozen.
7. Pack into large mason jars.

Penuche-in-a-Jar

This is the most requested candy at our house during the holidays!

Ingredients:

2	c. brown sugar
1	c. white sugar
1	c. cream
2	Tbs. light corn syrup
4	Tbs. butter
⅛	tsp. salt
1	tsp. vanilla extract
½	c. pecans, chopped, optional

Directions:

1. Butter an 8 x 8-inch square baking dish.
2. In medium saucepan, over medium heat, combine sugars, cream, corn syrup, butter, and salt. Stir until sugar is dissolved.
3. Boil to soft-ball stage, about 230 degrees F. on candy thermometer, until small amount of syrup dropped into cold water forms a soft ball.
4. Remove from heat; let cool while adding vanilla.
5. Beat until creamy, stir in nuts if desired.
6. Pour into prepared pan.
7. Let cool completely before cutting into squares.
8. Place in glass wide-mouth jar and seal with lid.

Yields: 1 pan, 8 x 8.

Peppermint Brittle-in-a-Jar

A true Christmas treat! The cool crunch of peppermint with creamy white chocolate is a divine combination.

Ingredients:

2	lb. white chocolate
30	sm. peppermint candy canes

Directions:

1. Line a baking sheet with waxed paper.
2. Place white chocolate in microwave-safe bowl.
3. Heat in microwave on medium setting for 5 to 6 minutes, stirring occasionally until chocolate is melted and smooth.
4. Place candy canes in plastic bag, or between two pieces of waxed paper.
5. Using a mallet or rolling pin, break candy canes into chunks.
6. Stir peppermint into melted white chocolate.
7. Spread evenly on pan; chill until set, about 1 hour.
8. Break into pieces and place into glass wide-mouth jar and seal with lid.

Yields: 36 servings.

Peppermint Taffy-in-a-Jar

Our kids enjoy making taffy and this candy tastes refreshing and is a great gift for the holidays. It is worth using a candy thermometer to get it correct.

Ingredients:

2	c. sugar
1	c. light corn syrup
1½	tsp. salt
1	c. water
2	Tbs. butter
¼	tsp. oil of peppermint
7	drops red food coloring

Directions:

1. Lightly butter a 15½ x 10½ x 1-inch baking pan.
2. In 2-quart saucepan, combine sugar, syrup, salt, and water.
3. Cook slowly, stirring constantly, until sugar dissolves.
4. Cook to hard-ball stage, 265 degrees F., without stirring.
5. Remove from heat; stir in remaining ingredients.
6. Pour into prepared baking pan.
7. Cool until comfortable to handle.
8. Butter hands; gather taffy into a ball, and pull.
9. When candy is light in color and gets hard to pull, cut in fourths; pull each piece into long strand about ½-inch thick.
10. With buttered scissors, quickly snip in bite-size pieces.
11. Wrap each piece in waxed paper and seal in jar.

Yields: 1¼ pounds individually wrapped taffy.

Salted Peanut Chews-in-a-Jar

These peanut chews never last very long at our house!

Ingredients:

1½	c. all-purpose flour
½	c. brown sugar, packed
¾	c. butter, softened, divided
3	c. miniature marshmallows
2	c. peanut butter flavored baking chips
⅔	c. corn syrup
2	tsp. vanilla extract
2	c. crisp rice cereal
2	c. salted peanuts

Directions:

1. Preheat oven to 350 degrees F.
2. In large mixing bowl, combine flour, brown sugar, and ½ cup softened butter.
3. Mix well and press into an ungreased 9 x 13-inch pan.
4. Bake 12 to 15 minutes or until lightly browned.
5. Sprinkle marshmallows over top and return to oven 3 to 5 minutes until marshmallows begin to melt; set aside.
6. In large saucepan, cook and stir peanut butter chips, corn syrup, vanilla, and remaining butter until chips are melted and smooth.
7. Remove from heat; stir in cereal and peanuts.
8. Pour over prepared crust, spreading to cover.
9. Cool before cutting into bars.
10. Place in glass wide-mouth jars and seal with lids.

Yields: 24 servings.

Turtle Candy-in-a-Jar

Pecans and caramel, smothered in melted chocolate – .....mmmmm!

Ingredients:

72	pecan halves
24	individually wrapped caramels, unwrapped
1	c. semisweet chocolate chips
2	tsp. shortening

Directions:

1. Preheat oven to 300 degrees F.
2. Grease baking sheets.
3. Place three pecan halves in a Y shape on cookie sheet and place caramel in center. Repeat with remaining nuts and caramels.
4. Place in preheated oven 10 minutes, until caramel is melted.
5. Melt chocolate chips with shortening in microwave, or in small saucepan over low heat; stir until smooth.
6. Spoon over candies on sheets. Chill 8 hours or overnight, until firm.
7. Place in glass wide-mouth canning jar and seal with lid.

Yields: 24 candies.

White Chocolate Covered
Pretzels-in-a-Jar

These are not only delicious; they make fun memories of time spent with your children helping!

Ingredients:

6	sq. white chocolate (1 oz.)
6	sq. dark chocolate (1 oz.)
2	pkg. mini twist pretzels (15 oz.)
½	c. red and green candy sprinkles, optional

Directions:

1. Melt white chocolate in top of double boiler, stirring constantly.
2. Dip pretzel halfway into white chocolate, completely covering half of the pretzel.
3. Roll in topping if desired, lay on wax paper.
4. Continue process until all white chocolate is finished. Place in refrigerator 15 minutes to harden.
5. Follow same process for dark chocolate pretzels.
6. Place in glass wide-mouth jars and seal with lids and rims.

Christmas Gifts-in-a-Jar Cookbook
A Collection of Christmas Gifts-in-a-Jar Recipes
Gifts-in-a-Jar Cookbook Series – Book 1

Cookies

Table of Contents

Page

Brownies Mix-in-a-Jar

All chocolate lovers will enjoy this treat. And they are great to have on hand during the holiday season.

Ingredients:

2¼	c. white sugar
⅔	c. unsweetened baking cocoa
1¼	c. all-purpose flour
1	tsp. baking powder
½	tsp. salt
¾	c. pecans, chopped

Directions:

1. Pour sugar into a clean and dry 1-quart jar; press down firmly.
2. Add cocoa powder and press down firmly.
3. Combine flour, baking powder, and salt; pour into jar and press down firmly.
4. Pour in chopped pecans, making sure pecans are evenly layered in the jar.

Directions for Tag

Additional Ingredients:

¾	c. butter, softened
4	eggs, slightly beaten

Directions:

1. Preheat oven to 350 degrees F.
2. Lightly grease or spray a 9 x 13-inch baking pan.
3. In large bowl, place jar of mix, using your hands to blend thoroughly.
4. Add butter and eggs, mixing until completely blended.
5. Spread batter into prepared baking pan.

6. Bake 30 minutes or until wooden toothpick inserted in center comes out clean.
7. Cool in pan.
8. Cut into 2-inch squares.

Yields: 2 dozen brownies.

Candy Bar Cookies Mix-in-a-Jar

This recipe lets you add your favorite candy bar to personalize your cookies to your own taste preference.

Ingredients:

½	c. white sugar
½	c. brown sugar
1	tsp. baking soda
2	c. all-purpose flour
1	c. your favorite candy bar, chopped

Directions:

1. Place white sugar into 1-quart wide-mouth canning jar, packing each layer in place before adding next ingredient.
2. Add brown sugar to jar, pack down.
3. Blend baking soda and flour together, add to jar.
4. Place chopped candy bar on top as last of layered ingredients.
5. Close jar and seal tightly.
6. Attach tag with mixing and baking directions.

Directions for Tag

Additional Ingredients:

¾	c. butter, softened
2	eggs, slightly beaten
1	tsp. vanilla extract

Directions:

1. Preheat oven to 350 degrees F.
2. In large bowl, cream butter, eggs, and vanilla together.
3. Add jar of cookie mix; stir together until mixture is well blended.

4.   Drop by rounded tablespoonfuls onto baking sheet.
5.   Cook 8 to 10 minutes, or until done.

Yields: 3 dozen cookies.

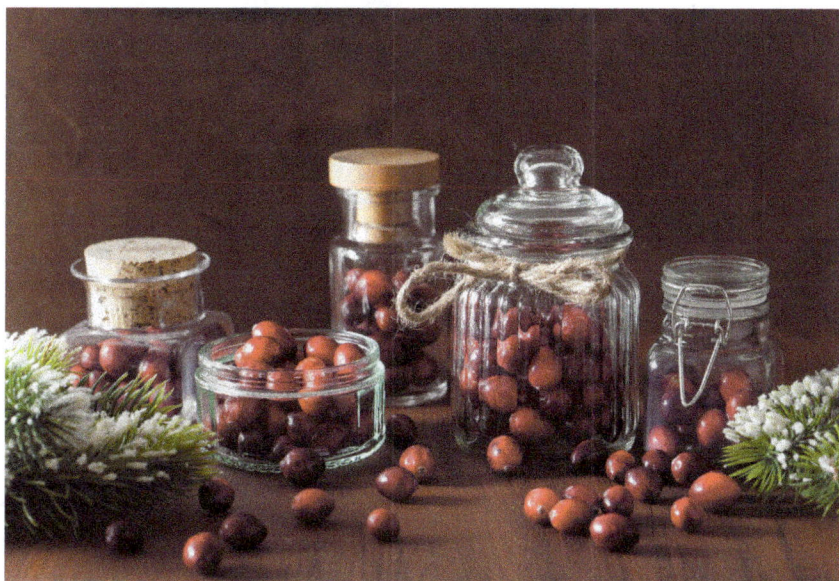

Candy-Coated Chocolate Cookies
Mix-in-a-Jar

These are delicious and visually appealing as well.

Ingredients:

½   tsp. baking soda
½   tsp. baking powder
2   c. all-purpose flour
1¼   c. sugar
1   c. candy-coated chocolate pcs.

Directions:

1.   In medium bowl, blend together baking soda, baking powder, and flour.
2.   Place flour mixture into 1-quart wide-mouth canning jar first; layer rest of ingredients into jar in order given, packing each layer in place before adding next ingredient.
3.   Attach directions for mixing and baking on tag.

Directions for Tag

Additional Ingredients:

¾   c. butter, softened
2   eggs, slightly beaten
1   tsp. vanilla extract

Directions:

1.   Preheat oven to 375 degrees F.
2.   In large bowl, cream butter, eggs, and vanilla together.
3.   Add cookie mix from jar; stir until mixture is well blended.
4.   Drop by rounded tablespoonfuls onto greased baking sheet.

5. Bake 10 to 12 minutes.
6. Transfer to wire racks to cool

Yields: 3 to 4 dozen cookies.

Chocolate Bar Oatmeal Cookies Mix-in-a-Jar

The combination of ground oatmeal and grated chocolate makes a deliciously flavored treat.

Ingredients:

1	c. all-purpose flour
½	tsp. baking powder
½	tsp. baking soda
1½	c. whole rolled oats
1	lg. chocolate bar
½	c. white sugar
½	c. brown sugar
½	c. nuts, chopped
½	c. semisweet chocolate chips

Directions:

1. In medium bowl, with wire whisk, mix together flour, baking powder, and baking soda.
2. Using a funnel with a wide opening, pour mixture into 1-quart wide-mouth jar, pack down level with a heavy object.
3. Process oatmeal in blender until finely ground.
4. Grate chocolate bar and mix into ground oatmeal.
5. Pack oatmeal mixture on top of flour in jar.
6. Add white sugar, pack down, add brown sugar, and pack down.
7. Layer chopped nuts on top of brown sugar.
8. Finish layering jar with chocolate chips until even with top; seal with a lid.
9. Attach tag with mixing and baking directions.

Directions for Tag

Additional Ingredients:

½	c. butter, softened
1	egg, lightly beaten
½	tsp. vanilla extract

Directions:

1. Preheat oven to 375 degrees F.
2. In small bowl, spoon chocolate chips and nuts, set aside.
3. In medium bowl, spoon brown and white sugar; add butter, cream well.
4. Add lightly beaten egg and vanilla, mix well.
5. Pour oatmeal and flour mixture from jar into bowl, mix thoroughly: stir in chocolate chips and nuts.
6. Roll into walnut-size balls, place on slightly greased baking sheet 2 inches apart
7. Bake 8 to 10 minutes, or until done.

Yields: 3 dozen cookies

Chocolate Chip Cookies Mix-in-a-Jar

This simple classic recipe is always a favorite.

Ingredients:

- 1¾ c. all-purpose flour
- ¾ tsp. baking soda
- ¾ tsp. salt
- 1½ c. chocolate chips (9 oz.)
- ¾ c. brown sugar
- ½ c. sugar

Directions:

1. In small bowl, combine flour, baking soda, and salt.
2. Place flour mixture into 1-quart wide-mouth canning jar first, layer remaining ingredients into jar in order given, packing each layer in place before adding next ingredient.
3. Close jar with a tight fitting lid.
4. Attach a gift card with the mixing and baking directions.

Directions for Tag

Additional Ingredients:

- ¾ c. butter, softened
- 1 egg, slightly beaten
- ¾ tsp. vanilla extract

Directions:

1. Preheat oven to 375 degrees F.
2. In large bowl, cream butter, egg, and vanilla together.
3. Add cookie mix from jar; stir until mixture is well blended.
4. Drop by rounded tablespoonfuls onto ungreased baking sheet.
5. Bake 9 to 11 minutes.

6. Transfer to wire racks to cool.
7. Note: Optional ½ cup of chopped nuts can be added to mixture.

Yields: 2 dozen cookies.

Chocolate-Covered Raisin Cookies
Mix-in-a-Jar

Chocolate-covered raisins make a wonderful flavor addition to these cookies.

Ingredients:

2	c. all-purpose flour
1	tsp. baking powder
¼	c. brown sugar
1¼	c. chocolate covered raisins
¾	c. sugar
¼	c. semisweet chocolate chips

Directions:

1. In medium bowl, blend together baking powder and flour.
2. Place flour mixture into 1-quart wide-mouth canning jar first, layer remaining ingredients into jar in order given, packing each layer in place before adding next ingredient.
3. Attach gift card with mixing and baking directions.

Directions for Tag

Additional Ingredients:

½	c. butter, softened
2	eggs, slightly beaten
1¼	tsp. vanilla extract

Directions:

1. Preheat oven to 375 degrees F.
2. Lightly grease a baking sheet.
3. In large bowl, cream butter, eggs, and vanilla together.
4. Add cookie mix from jar; stir until mixture is blended.

5. Drop by rounded tablespoonfuls onto prepared baking sheet.
6. Bake 10 to 13 minutes.
7. Transfer to wire racks to cool.

Yields: 3 dozen cookies.

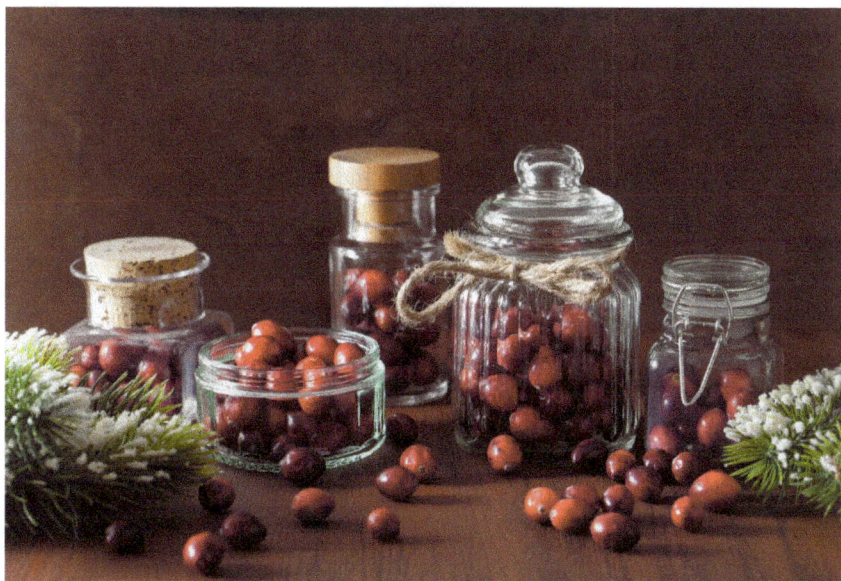

Chocolate Pecan Chewies Mix-in-a-Jar

Chocolate and pecans make a great combination in this cookie mix.

Ingredients:

1¾	c. all-purpose flour
1	tsp. baking soda
1	c. sugar
⅓	c. brown sugar, firmly packed
½	c. cocoa powder
1	c. pecans, chopped

Directions:

1. In small bowl, blend together flour and soda.
2. Layer ingredients in order given into 1-quart wide-mouth canning jar.
3. Pack each layer in place before adding next ingredient.
4. Attach a gift card with mixing and baking directions.

Directions for Tag

Additional Ingredients:

1	stick butter, softened
1	egg, slightly beaten
1	tsp. vanilla extract

Directions:

1. Preheat oven to 375 degrees F.
2. Lightly grease a baking sheet.
3. In large bowl, use your hands to thoroughly mix.
4. Add butter, egg, and vanilla and continue mixing with your hands.
5. Shape into balls the size of walnuts.
6. Place 2 inches apart onto prepared baking sheet.

7. Bake 11 to 13 minutes.
8. Transfer to wire racks to cool.

Yields: 1 dozen cookies.

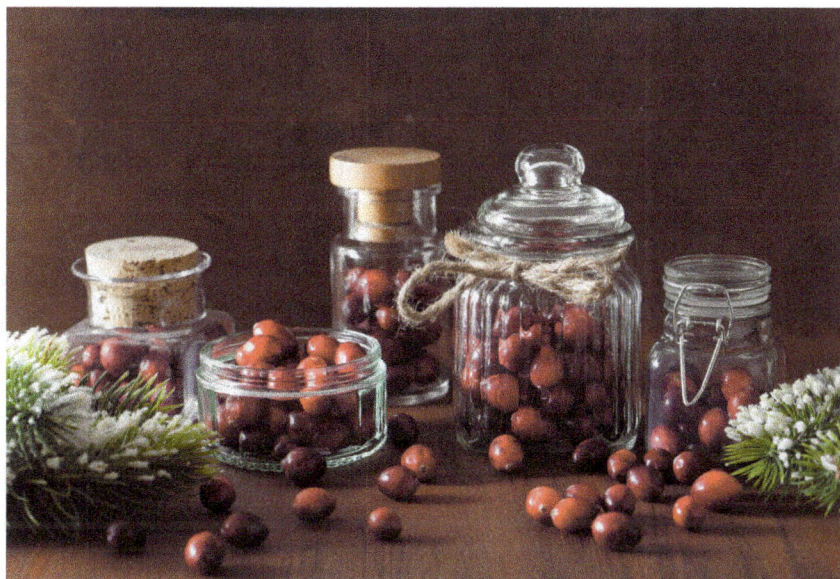

Chunky Butterscotch Cookies
Mix-in-a-Jar

Butterscotch and pecans together yield deliciously aromatic and flavorful cookies.

Ingredients:

- 1¾ c. all-purpose flour
- 1 tsp. baking soda
- 1 tsp. baking powder
- ¾ c. brown sugar
- 1 tsp. ground cinnamon
- ½ c. sugar
- 1 c. butterscotch baking chips
- ½ c. pecans, chopped

Directions:

1. In medium bowl, blend together flour, baking soda, and baking powder.
2. Place flour mixture into 1-quart wide-mouth canning jar first, layer remaining ingredients into jar in order given, packing each layer in place before adding next ingredient.
3. Attach gift card with mixing and baking directions.

Directions for Tag

Additional Ingredients:

- ¾ c. butter, softened
- 3 eggs, slightly beaten
- 1 tsp. vanilla extract

Directions:

1. Preheat oven to 375 degrees F.
2. Lightly grease a baking sheet.
3. In large bowl, cream butter, eggs, and vanilla together.
4. Add jar of cookie mix and stir until mixture is well blended.
5. Drop by rounded tablespoonfuls onto prepared baking sheet.
6. Bake 11 to 13 minutes.
7. Transfer to wire racks to cool.

Chunky Chocolate Cookies
Mix-in-a-Jar

If you like a big, chunky cookie chock full of nuts and chunks of chocolate, this is the recipe for you!

Ingredients:

1	tsp. baking soda
1	tsp. baking powder
1¾	c. all-purpose flour
¾	c. brown sugar
½	c. sugar
¼	c. baking cocoa powder
½	c. pecans, chopped
1	c. chocolate chips or chunks

Directions:

1. In medium bowl, blend together baking soda, baking powder, and flour.
2. Place flour mixture into 1-quart wide-mouth canning jar first, layer remaining ingredients into jar in order given, packing each layer in place before adding next ingredient.
3. Attach a gift card with mixing and baking directions.

Directions for Tag

Additional Ingredients:

¾	c. butter, softened
3	eggs, slightly beaten
1	tsp. vanilla extract

Directions:

1. Preheat oven to 350 degrees F.
2. Lightly grease a baking sheet.
3. In large bowl, cream butter, eggs, and vanilla together.
4. Add mix from jar and stir until mixture is well blended.
5. Drop by rounded tablespoonfuls onto prepared baking sheet.
6. Bake 11 to 13 minutes.
7. Transfer to wire racks to cool.

Yields: 3 dozen cookies.

Festive Fruitcake Bars-in-a-Jar

These fruitcake bars with candied fruit and pecans are a delicious holiday treat.

Ingredients:

1½	c. all-purpose flour
½	c. granulated sugar
¼	c. light brown sugar, packed
¾	c. milk
½	c. butter, softened
2	eggs
1	tsp. vanilla extract
½	tsp. baking powder
½	tsp. cinnamon
¼	tsp. ground nutmeg
¼	tsp. allspice
1½	c. mixed candied fruits and peels (12 oz.)
1	c. pecans, chopped
8	oz. dates, chopped
	zest of 1 lemon

Directions:

1. Preheat oven to 350 degrees F.
2. Grease and flour a 15 x 10-inch jellyroll pan.
3. In large mixing bowl, measure flour, sugars, milk, butter, eggs, vanilla, baking powder, and spices.
4. At low speed, beat ingredients just until blended.
5. Increase speed to high and beat 3 minutes, scraping bottom and sides of bowl occasionally.
6. Stir in candied fruits and peels, pecans, dates, and lemon zest. Spread batter into prepared pan.
7. Bake 40 to 45 minutes or until a wooden toothpick inserted in center comes out clean.

8.   Cool in pan on wire rack. Cut into 3 x 1-inch bars.

9.   Store in tightly covered container for up to 1 week.

Yields: 50 bars.

Directions for Tag

1.   Enjoy this treat right from the jar.

Hazelnut Cookies Mix-in-a-Jar

This is a crispy crunchy cookie, great for gift giving or receiving.

Ingredients:

½	tsp. baking powder
½	tsp. baking soda
¾	c. all-purpose flour
¾	c. old-fashioned oats
¼	c. brown sugar
¾	c. hazelnuts, chopped
¼	c. brown sugar
1	c. rice cereal, crisped
½	c. sugar

Directions:

1. In small bowl, blend together baking powder, baking soda, and flour.
2. Place flour mixture into 1-quart wide-mouth canning jar first, layer remaining ingredients into jar in order given, packing each layer in place before adding next ingredient.
3. Attach directions for mixing and baking on tag.

Directions for Tag

Additional Ingredients:

½	c. butter, softened
2	eggs, slightly beaten
1¼	tsp. vanilla extract

Directions:

1. Preheat oven to 350 degrees F.
2. Lightly grease a baking sheet.
3. In large bowl, cream butter, eggs, and vanilla together.
4. Add hazelnut cookie mix from jar and stir until mixture is well blended.
5. Drop by rounded tablespoonfuls onto prepared baking sheet.
6. Bake 10 to 12 minutes.
7. Transfer to wire racks to cool.

Yields: 3 to 4 dozen cookies.

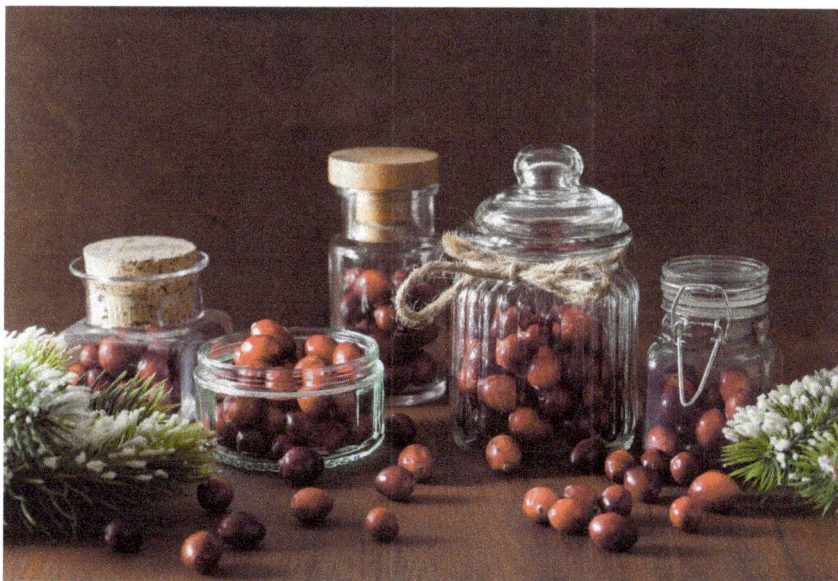

Molasses Cookies Mix-in-a-Jar

I am a fan of molasses cookies, and this cookie mix makes a nice gift.

Ingredients:

1⅓	c. sugar
1	tsp. baking soda
1	tsp. baking powder
1¼	tsp. cinnamon
½	tsp. nutmeg
¼	tsp. cloves
⅛	tsp. allspice
1	tsp. ginger
3	c. all-purpose flour

Directions:

1. Layer ingredients in order given into 1-quart wide-mouth canning jar.
2. Pack each layer in place before adding next ingredient.
3. Attach a gift card with mixing and baking directions.

Directions for Tag

Additional Ingredients:

¾	c. butter, softened
2	eggs, slightly beaten
¼	c. sweet molasses

Directions:

1. Preheat oven to 375 degrees F.
2. Lightly grease a baking sheet.
3. In large bowl, cream butter, eggs, and molasses together.
4. Add cookie mix from jar and stir until mixture is well blended.
5. Drop by rounded tablespoonfuls onto prepared baking sheet.
6. Bake 10 to 12 minutes.
7. Transfer to wire racks to cool.

Yields: 3 dozen cookies.

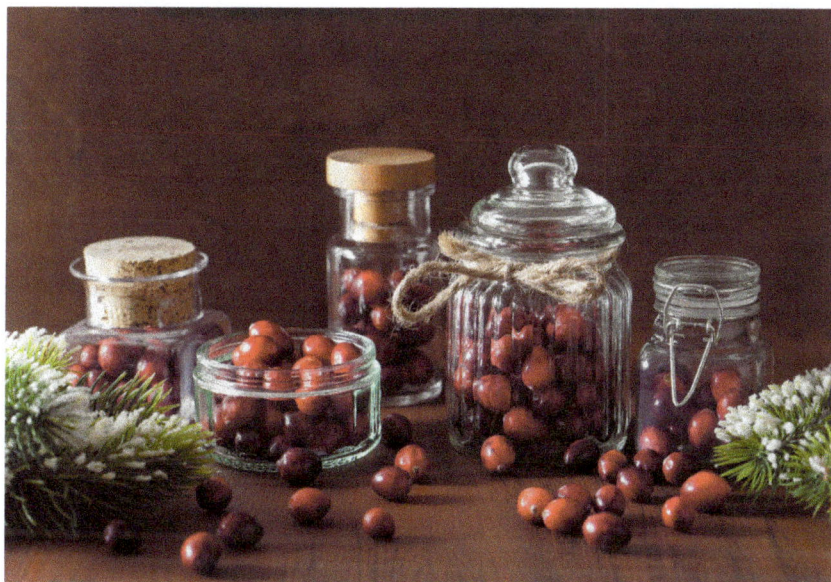

Oatmeal Butterscotch Cookies
Mix-in-a-Jar

This is the traditional butterscotch oatmeal cookie that I grew up with. I hope you enjoy them as well.

Ingredients:

1	tsp. baking soda
1	c. all-purpose flour
¾	c. brown sugar
½	c. sugar
½	c. butterscotch baking chips
2	c. old-fashioned oats
1¼	tsp. ground cinnamon

Directions:

1. In small bowl, blend together baking soda and flour.
2. Place flour mixture into 1-quart wide-mouth canning jar first, layer remaining ingredients into jar in order given, packing each layer in place before adding next ingredient.
3. Attach directions for mixing and baking on the tag.

Directions for Tag

Additional Ingredients:

¾	c. butter, softened
2	eggs, slightly beaten
1¼	tsp. vanilla extract

Directions:

1. Preheat oven to 350 degrees F.
2. Lightly grease a baking sheet.
3. In large bowl, cream butter, eggs, and vanilla together.
4. Add cookie mix and stir until mixture is well blended.
5. Drop by rounded tablespoonfuls onto prepared baking sheet.
6. Bake 10 to 12 minutes.
7. Transfer to wire racks to cool.

Yields: 3 dozen cookies.

Oatmeal Chocolate Cookies
Mix-in-a-Jar

This is one of my favorite recipes, especially for a late-night treat.

Ingredients:

1	tsp. baking soda
1	c. all-purpose flour
¾	c. brown sugar
½	c. sugar
½	c. chocolate baking chips
2	c. old-fashioned oats
1¼	Tbs. cinnamon, ground

Directions:

1. In medium bowl, blend together baking soda and flour.
2. Place flour mixture into 1-quart wide-mouth canning jar first, layer remaining ingredients into jar in order given, packing each layer in place before adding next ingredient.
3. Attach directions for mixing and baking on tag.

Directions for Tag

Additional Ingredients:

¾	c. butter, softened
2	eggs, slightly beaten
1¼	tsp. vanilla extract

Directions:

1. Preheat oven to 350 degrees F.
2. Lightly grease a baking sheet.
3. In large bowl cream butter, eggs, and vanilla together.
4. Add cookie mix and stir until mixture is well blended.
5. Drop by rounded tablespoonfuls onto prepared baking sheet.
6. Bake 10 to 12 minutes.
7. Transfer to wire racks to cool.

Yields: 3 to 4 dozen cookies.

Oatmeal, Cranberry, and Spice Cookies Mix-in-a-Jar

This recipe makes fruity, spicy cookies that are very aromatic and hard to resist.

Ingredients:

1	tsp. baking soda
2	c. all-purpose flour
½	c. dried cranberries, chopped
½	c. sugar
1	tsp. ground cinnamon
½	tsp. ground nutmeg
½	c. brown sugar
1¼	c. old-fashioned oats

Directions:

1. In medium bowl, blend together baking soda and flour.
2. Place flour mixture into 1-quart wide-mouth canning jar first, layer remaining ingredients into jar in order given, packing each layer in place before adding next ingredient.
3. Attach directions for mixing and baking on tag.

Directions for Tag

Additional Ingredients:

¾	c. butter, softened
2	eggs, slightly beaten
1	tsp. vanilla extract

Directions:

1. Preheat oven to 350 degrees F.
2. Lightly grease a baking sheet.
3. In large bowl, cream butter, eggs, and vanilla together.
4. Add cookie mix from jar and stir until mixture is well blended.
5. Drop by rounded tablespoonfuls onto prepared baking sheet.
6. Bake 10 to 12 minutes.
7. Transfer to wire racks to cool.

Yields: 3 to 4 dozen cookies.

Orange Slice Cookies Mix-in-a-Jar

These make an attractive variation for a gift-in-a-jar. Decorate your jar with a big orange and white ribbon to make it even more attractive.

Ingredients:

- ½ tsp. baking soda
- 1 tsp. baking powder
- 1¾ c. all-purpose flour
- ¾ c. sugar
- ½ c. brown sugar
- 1½ c. sugar coated orange slice candies, quartered, and wrapped in plastic wrap or sealed in a baggie

Directions:

1. In medium bowl, blend together baking soda, baking powder, and flour.
2. Place flour mixture into 1-quart wide-mouth canning jar first, layer remaining ingredients into jar in order given, packing each layer in place before adding next ingredient, ending with wrapped candies on top.
3. Attach directions for mixing and baking to tag.

Directions for Tag

Additional Ingredients:

- ½ c. butter softened
- 2 eggs, slightly beaten
- 1 tsp. vanilla extract

Directions:

1. Preheat oven to 375 degrees F.
2. Lightly grease a baking sheet.
3. In large bowl, cream butter, eggs, and vanilla together.
4. Remove orange slice candies from jar and set aside.
5. Add mix from jar and stir until mixture is well blended.
6. Stir in orange slice candies.
7. Drop by rounded tablespoonfuls onto prepared baking sheet.
8. Bake 12 to 14 minutes.
9. Transfer to wire racks to cool.

Yields: 3 to 4 dozen cookies.

Peanut Butter Chocolate Chip Cookies
Mix-in-a-Jar

These are easy-to-make cookies and the chocolate chips always make them popular.

Ingredients:

½	tsp. baking soda
2	c. all-purpose flour
¾	c. brown sugar
¾	c. sugar
1	c. chocolate chips

Directions:

1. In medium bowl, blend together baking soda and flour.
2. Place flour mixture into 1-quart wide-mouth canning jar first, layer remaining ingredients into jar in order given, packing each layer in place before adding next ingredient.
3. Attach directions for mixing and baking to tag.

Directions for Tag

Additional Ingredients:

1	c. butter, softened
2	eggs, slightly beaten
1¼	tsp. vanilla extract
1	c. creamy peanut butter

Directions:

1. Preheat oven to 350 degrees F.
2. Lightly grease a baking sheet.
3. In large bowl, cream butter, eggs, and vanilla together.
4. Blend in peanut butter.
5. Add mix from jar and stir until mixture is well blended.
6. Drop by rounded tablespoonfuls onto prepared baking sheet.
7. Bake 9 to 11 minutes.
8. Transfer to wire racks to cool.

Yields: 3 to 4 dozen cookies.

Peanut Butter Cookies Mix-in-a-Jar

The combination of peanuts and peanut butter chips are a pleasing texture in this old classic.

Ingredients:

1	tsp. baking soda
1½	c. all-purpose flour
¾	c. salted peanuts, chopped
¾	c. brown sugar
¾	c. sugar
1	c. peanut butter chips

Directions:

1. In small bowl, blend together baking soda and flour.
2. Place flour mixture into 1-quart wide-mouth canning jar first, layer remaining ingredients into jar in order given, packing each layer in place before adding next ingredient.
3. Attach directions for mixing and baking to tag.

Directions for Tag

Additional Ingredients:

½	c. butter, softened
1	egg, slightly beaten
1	tsp. vanilla extract
½	c. creamy peanut butter

Directions:

1. Preheat oven to 350 degrees F.
2. Lightly grease a baking sheet.
3. In large bowl, cream butter, egg, and vanilla together.
4. Blend in peanut butter.
5. Add mix from jar and stir until mixture is well blended.

6. Drop by rounded tablespoonfuls onto prepared baking sheet.
7. Bake 11 to 13 minutes.
8. Transfer to wire racks to cool.

Yields: 3 to 4 dozen cookies.

Pecan White Chocolate Chip
Cookies Mix-in-a-Jar

Oatmeal, pecans, and white chocolate chips make an attractive gift-in-a-jar that is also very tasty.

Ingredients:

½	tsp. baking soda
½	tsp. baking powder
¾	c. all-purpose flour
¾	c. old-fashioned oats
¾	c. pecans, chopped
1	c. white chocolate chips
½	c. brown sugar
½	c. sugar

Directions:

1. In small bowl, blend together baking soda, baking powder, and flour.
2. Place flour mixture into 1-quart wide-mouth canning jar first, layer remaining ingredients into jar in order given, packing each layer in place before adding next ingredient.
3. Attach a gift card with mixing and baking directions.

Directions for Tag

Additional Ingredients:

½	c. butter, softened
2	eggs, slightly beaten
1¼	tsp. vanilla extract

Directions:

1. Preheat oven to 350 degrees F.
2. Lightly grease a baking sheet.
3. In large bowl, cream butter, eggs, and vanilla together.
4. Add mix from jar and stir until mixture is well blended.
5. Drop by rounded tablespoonfuls onto prepared baking sheet.
6. Bake 10 to 12 minutes.
7. Transfer to wire racks to cool.

Yields: 3 to 4 dozen cookies.

Snicker Doodle Cookies
Mix-in-a-Jar

Snicker Doodles are one of my nephew's favorite cookies and this is an easy to make version.

Ingredients:

1	tsp. baking soda
2	tsp. cream of tartar
2¾	c. all-purpose flour
¼	c. brown sugar
1¼	c. sugar

Directions:

1. In large bowl, blend together baking soda, cream of tartar, and flour.
2. Place flour mixture into 1-quart wide-mouth canning jar first, layer remaining ingredients into jar in order given, packing each layer in place before adding next ingredient.
3. Attach a gift card with mixing and baking directions.

Directions for Tag

Additional Ingredients:

1	c. butter, softened
2	eggs, slightly beaten
½	c. sugar
1¼	Tbs. cinnamon

Directions:

1. Preheat oven to 375 degrees F.
2. In large bowl, cream butter until light, add eggs and beat until mixture is smooth.
3. Add cookie mix from jar and continue to beat until dough begins to form.
4. In small bowl, combine sugar and cinnamon.
5. Shape dough into 1-inch balls and roll in cinnamon sugar blend.
6. Arrange on ungreased baking sheet.
7. Bake 10 to 15 minutes or until light tan.
8. Transfer to wire racks to cool.

Yields: 4 to 5 dozen cookies.

Toffee Candy Bar Cookies Mix-in-a-Jar

Toffee candy bars have been very popular for years, and this recipe for a mix-in-a-jar makes a great gift and great cookies.

Ingredients:

1	tsp. baking soda
2	c. all-purpose flour
½	c. sugar
½	c. brown sugar
1	c. toffee candy bars, coarsely chopped

Directions:

1. In medium bowl, blend together baking soda and flour.
2. Place flour mixture into 1-quart wide-mouth canning jar first, layer remaining ingredients into jar in order given, packing each layer in place before adding next ingredient.
3. Attach directions for mixing and baking on tag.

Directions for Tag

Additional Ingredients:

¾	c. butter, softened
2	eggs, slightly beaten
1	tsp. vanilla extract

Directions:

1. Preheat oven to 350 degrees F.
2. Lightly grease a baking sheet.
3. In large bowl, cream butter, eggs, and vanilla together.
4. Add cookie mix from jar and stir until mixture is well blended.
5. Drop by rounded tablespoonfuls onto prepared baking sheet.

6. Bake 10 to 12 minutes.
7. Transfer to wire racks to cool.

Yields: 3 to 4 dozen cookies.

Trail Mix Cookies Mix-in-a-Jar

These make a nutritious cookie. Make sure you use fresh wheat germ and keep refrigerated until ready to use.

Ingredients:

1	tsp. baking powder
¾	c. all-purpose flour
½	c. brown sugar
½	c. sugar
¾	c. wheat germ
½	c. rolled oats
1	c. raisins
⅓	c. coconut, flaked
¾	c. pecans, chopped

Directions:

1. In small bowl, blend together baking powder and flour.
2. Place flour mixture into 1-quart wide-mouth canning jar first, layer remaining ingredients into jar in order given, packing each layer in place before adding next ingredient.
3. Attach a gift card with mixing and baking directions.

Directions for Tag

Ingredients:

½	c. butter, softened
2	eggs, slightly beaten
1¼	tsp. vanilla extract

Directions:

1. Preheat oven to 350 degrees F.
2. Lightly grease a baking sheet.
3. In large bowl, cream butter, eggs, and vanilla together.
4. Add mix in jar and stir until mixture is well blended.
5. Drop by rounded tablespoonfuls onto prepared baking sheet.
6. Bake 12 to 14 minutes.
7. Transfer to wire racks to cool.

Yields: 3 to 4 dozen.

Triple Chocolate Chip Cookies
Mix-in-a-Jar

Two kinds of chocolate chips blend with cocoa for a triple chocolate cookie. Chocolate lovers love these!

Ingredients:

1¼	c. all-purpose flour
½	tsp. baking soda
2	Tbs. plus 2 tsp. cocoa powder
6	Tbs. sugar
⅓	c. brown sugar
½	c. white chocolate chips
¾	c. pecans, chopped
½	c. chocolate chips

Directions:

1. In small bowl, blend together flour and baking soda.
2. Place flour mixture into 1-quart wide-mouth canning jar first, layer remaining ingredients into jar in order given, packing each layer in place before adding next ingredient.
3. Attach a gift card with mixing and baking directions.

Directions for Tag

Additional Ingredients:

½	c. butter, softened
2	eggs, slightly beaten
1	Tbs. cream
1¼	tsp. vanilla extract

Directions:

1. Preheat oven to 350 degrees F.
2. Lightly grease a baking sheet.
3. In large bowl, cream butter, eggs, milk, and vanilla together.
4. Add mix from jar and stir until mixture is well blended.
5. Drop by rounded tablespoonfuls onto prepared baking sheet.
6. Bake 8 to 10 minutes.
7. Transfer to wire racks to cool.

Yields: 3 to 4 dozen cookies.

Vanilla and Chocolate Chip Cookies
Mix-in-a-Jar

The blend of chocolate chips makes a tasty chocolate treat.

Ingredients:

2	c. all-purpose flour
1	tsp. baking soda
1	tsp baking powder
⅓	c. brown sugar
⅔	c. sugar
1	c. semisweet chocolate chips
½	c. white chocolate chips

Directions:

1. In large bowl, blend together flour, baking soda, and baking powder.
2. Place flour mixture into 1-quart wide-mouth canning jar first, layer remaining ingredients into jar in order given, packing each layer in place before adding next ingredient.
3. Attach a gift card with mixing and baking directions.

Directions for Tag

Additional Ingredients:

¾	c. butter, softened
2	eggs, slightly beaten
1¼	tsp. vanilla extract

Directions:

1. Preheat oven to 350 degrees F.
2. Lightly grease a baking sheet.
3. In large bowl, cream butter, eggs, and vanilla together.
4. Add mix from jar and stir until mixture is well blended.
5. Drop by rounded tablespoonfuls onto prepared baking sheet.
6. Bake 15 to 18 minutes.
7. Transfer to wire racks to cool.

Yields: 3 to 4 dozen cookies.

White Chocolate Macadamia Nut Cookies
Mix-in-a-Jar

This is a tasty, melt-in-your-mouth cookie, using delicious macadamia nuts and white chocolate chunks.

Ingredients:

2	c. all-purpose flour
½	tsp. baking soda
½	tsp. baking powder
1¼	c. sugar
¾	c. macadamia nuts, chopped
1	c. white chocolate chunks

Directions:

1. In large bowl, blend together flour, baking soda, and baking powder.
2. Place flour mixture into 1-quart wide-mouth canning jar first, layer remaining ingredients into jar in order given, packing each layer in place before adding next ingredient.
3. Attach a gift tag with mixing and baking directions.

Directions for Tag

Additional Ingredients:

1	c. butter, softened
2	eggs, slightly beaten
2	tsp. vanilla extract

Directions:

1. Preheat oven to 375 degrees F.
2. Lightly grease a baking sheet.
3. In large bowl, cream butter, eggs, and vanilla together.
4. Add mix from jar and stir until mixture is well blended.
5. Drop by rounded tablespoonfuls onto prepared baking sheet.
6. Bake 12 to 14 minutes.
7. Transfer to wire racks to cool.

Yields: 3 to 4 dozen cookies.

Christmas Gifts-in-a-Jar Cookbook
A Collection of Christmas Gifts-in-a-Jar Recipes
Gifts-in-a-Jar Cookbook Series – Book 1

Dressings, Sauces, and Condiments

Table of Contents

Page

Bread Coating Mix-in-a-Jar

This makes a flavorful coating to give as a gift-in-a-jar.

Ingredients:

3¼	c. dry bread crumbs, crushed
⅓	c. flour
6	Tbs. paprika
4	tsp. salt
2	tsp. onion powder
2	tsp. ground oregano
1	tsp. ground red pepper
¾	tsp. garlic powder
¼	c. dried parsley flakes

Directions:

1. Mix dry ingredients together in 1-quart jar.
2. Store in tightly covered container.

Yields: 4 cups mix.

Directions for Tag

Additional Ingredients:

⅓	c. butter, melted
	milk
	your choice chicken, pork chops or fish

Directions:

1. Preheat oven to 400 degrees F.
2. Dip chicken into milk with melted butter to coat, dip into coating.
3. Arrange in a single layer in ungreased shallow baking dish.
4. Bake 50 to 60 minutes or until tender and brown.
5. Use the same method for pork chops or fish and bake until done.

Cajun Spice Seasoning Mix-in-a-Jar

This makes a great gift for those who enjoy the flavors of Cajun foods.

Ingredients for mix:

¾	c. salt
¼	c. ground cayenne pepper
2	Tbs. ground white pepper
2	Tbs. ground black pepper
2	Tbs. paprika
2	Tbs. onion powder
2	Tbs. garlic powder

Directions:

1. While holding a pint canning jar at an angle, add ingredients to create a "sand art" look. The salt and cayenne may be divided into smaller portions and used to separate other spices. I found it simplest to use 7 cups (one with each spice in it) and add them to my jar with a spoon, as I want to create the special look.
2. Place in a small, pretty jar tied with a ribbon.

Directions for Tag

1. Use to taste for seasoning chicken, seafood, steak, or vegetables.

Creole Seasoning Mix-in-a-Jar

This makes a tasty gift for those who enjoy the flavors of Creole or Cajun foods.

Ingredients:

3	Tbs. paprika
2	Tbs. garlic powder
1	Tbs. salt
1	Tbs. onion powder
1	Tbs. dried oregano
1	Tbs. dried thyme
1	Tbs. cayenne pepper
1	Tbs. pepper

Directions:

1. Combine all ingredients.
2. Place into pretty jar tied with a ribbon.

Yield: ½ cup.

Directions for Tag

1. Use Creole Seasoning Mix to season chicken, seafood, steak or vegetables.

Dried Apricot-Cherry Chutney-in-a-Jar

The great flavor of apricots, apples, and cherries combine to make a delicious apple chutney and a great Christmas gift.

Ingredients:

1¼	c. cider vinegar
1	c. dry white wine
1	c. brown sugar
1	tsp. sea salt
½	tsp. hot red chili flakes
2	Tbs. crystallized ginger, chopped
3	star anise, whole
2	tsp. coriander seed, whole
½	tsp. black pepper, freshly ground
2	Tbs. fresh garlic, slivered
1½	c. dried apricots, quartered (about 6 oz.)
2	c. dried tart cherries (about 5 oz.)
1½	lb. tart sweet apples (Fuji or Gala), peeled, cut in lg. dice

Ingredients:

1. In large non-aluminum saucepan, place all ingredients except apples; bring to a boil.
2. Reduce heat; simmer partially covered for 10 minutes.
3. Add apples and bring to a boil; reduce heat and simmer partially covered 35 minutes until mixture has thickened, stirring occasionally.
4. Remove and discard star anise if desired.
5. Ladle into hot sterilized jars, seal, and refrigerate.
6. Keeps up to 3 months refrigerated.

Yields: 3 cups.

Enchilada Spice Mix-in-a-Jar

Fragrant spices combine to flavor your favorite enchiladas. Enjoy!

Ingredients:

1	tsp. salt
1	tsp. chili powder
½	tsp. sugar
½	tsp. ground cumin
¼	tsp. oregano
2	tsp. dried minced onion
1	tsp. dried chili pepper
1	tsp. corn meal
½	tsp. dried minced garlic
1	tsp. paprika

Directions:

1. In medium bowl, combine all ingredients.
2. Place into a pretty jar tied with a ribbon.

Yield: ½ cup.

Directions for Tag

1. In small bowl, mix together with a little water and a squeeze of lime juice, use amount you desire.
2. Add to your favorite enchiladas.

Favorite Fish Seasoning
Mix-in-a-Jar

Our family loves fish and this makes a great tasting fish seasoning mix.

Ingredients:

2½	c. yellow cornmeal
1¼	c. all-purpose flour
3	tsp. paprika
2	tsp. dried parsley flakes, crushed
1	tsp. salt
1½	tsp. celery salt
1½	tsp. onion salt
1	tsp. lemon pepper
½	tsp. ground red pepper

Directions:

1. In large bowl, combine all ingredients and mix well.
2. Store in glass jar.

Yields: 3¾ cups mix, should coat 4 pounds fresh fish.

Directions for Tag

Additional Ingredients:

1	egg
1	c. buttermilk
4	lb. fish (your favorite variety)
	canola oil, for frying

Directions:

1. In deep skillet, heat 1½ inches of canola oil to 375 degrees F.
2. In small bowl, combine egg and buttermilk.
3. Dip fish into egg mixture.
4. Place seasoning mix in a bag and shake dipped fish pieces one by one, until well coated.
5. Fry until fish is golden brown and flakes easily with fork.
6. Drain on paper towels and serve.

Hazelnut Raspberry Vinaigrette-in-a-Jar

This vinaigrette really is exceptional and makes great gifts!

Ingredients:

½	c. fresh raspberries, puréed
1	c. raspberry vinegar
2	Tbs. sugar
3	Tbs. corn syrup
2	c. hazelnut oil
¼	c. hazelnuts, roasted and crushed

Directions:

1. In small bowl, combine first 4 ingredients.
2. Slowly drizzle oil into mixture while whipping.
3. Stir in nuts to finish.

Directions for Tag

1. Use to taste for seasoning pork, steak, or vegetables.

Hot Shot Cherries-in-a-Jar

These pecans and cherries pack a punch!

Ingredients:

2	c. pecan halves
1	c. dried tart cherries
2	Tbs. Worcestershire sauce
½-1	tsp. cayenne pepper, or to taste
½	tsp. garlic powder
½-1	tsp. seasoned salt, or to taste
½	tsp. ground cumin
⅛	tsp. dried oregano
1-2	Tbs. canola oil

Directions:

1. In medium bowl, combine pecans and cherries.
2. In small bowl, combine Worcestershire sauce, cayenne, garlic powder, seasoned salt, cumin, and oregano; mix well.
3. Pour over pecan mixture; stir to coat.
4. Heat oil in large skillet over medium heat.
5. Add pecan mixture and cook, stirring constantly, 4 to 5 minutes. Do not allow mixture to burn.
6. Remove from heat.
7. Spread pecans on wax paper to cool.
8. Place cooled nut mixture into jars.

Yields: 3 cups.

Old Bay Seasoning Mix-in-a-Jar

Traditional old bay spice makes a fragrant Christmas gift. Enjoy!

Ingredients:

1	Tbs. ground bay leaves
2½	tsp. celery salt
1½	tsp. dry mustard
1½	tsp. black pepper
¾	tsp. ground nutmeg
½	tsp. ground cloves
½	tsp. ground ginger
½	tsp. paprika
½	tsp. red pepper
¼	tsp. ground mace
¼	tsp. ground cardamom

Directions:

1. In small bowl, combine all ingredients.
2. Store in an airtight container.

Directions for Tag

1. Attach a card with the following statement:
   Old Bay Seasoning Mix is great to season the flour for fried chicken, and on French fries as well as for use with seafood.

Ranch Dressing and Dip Mix-in-a-Jar

This versatile mix can be used to make dressing for salads, a dip for fresh veggies, or topping for baked potatoes.

Ingredients:

3	Tbs.	dried parsley
1	Tbs.	dried chives
½	Tbs.	dried tarragon
1	Tbs.	lemon pepper
2	Tbs.	salt
½	Tbs.	oregano
¼	Tbs.	garlic powder

Directions:

1. In medium bowl, combine all ingredients.
2. Store in an airtight jar.

Directions for Tag

Ingredients:

2	Tbs.	Ranch Dressing and Dip Mix
1	c.	mayonnaise
1	c.	buttermilk

Directions:

1. In large bowl, whisk together Ranch Dressing and Dip Mix, mayonnaise, and buttermilk.
2. Refrigerate for 2 hours before serving with snack crackers, breadsticks, fresh vegetables, or as topping for your favorite salad or baked potatoes.

Yields: 2 cups

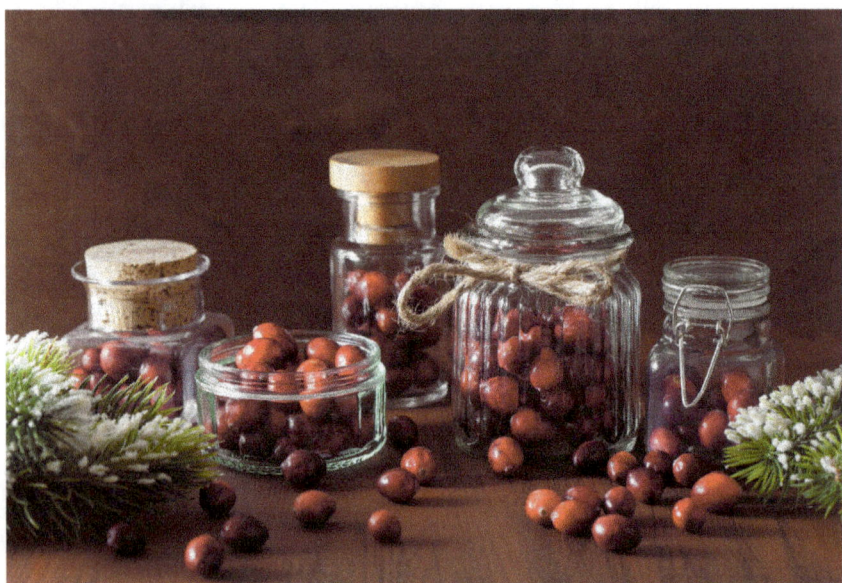

Christmas Gifts-in-a-Jar Cookbook
A Collection of Christmas Gifts-in-a-Jar Recipes
Gifts-in-a-Jar Cookbook Series – Book 1

Jams, Jellies, and Syrups

Table of Contents

A Basic Guide for Canning Jams, Jellies, and Syrups

1. Wash jars in hot, soapy water inside and out with brush or soft cloth.
2. Run your finger around the rim of each jar, discarding any with cracks or chips.
3. Rinse well in clean, clear, hot water using tongs to avoid burns to hands or fingers.
4. Place upside down on clean cloth to drain well.
5. Place lids in boiling water for 2 minutes to sterilize and keep hot until placing on rim of jar.
6. Immediately prior to filling each jar, immerse in very hot water with tongs to heat jar. (avoids breakage of jar with hot liquid)
7. Fill jar to within 1 inch of top of rim.
8. Wipe rim with clean damp cloth to remove any particles of food and check again for any chips or cracks.
9. With tongs place lid from hot bath directly onto rim of jar.
10. Using gloves, cloth, or holders tighten lid firmly onto jar with ring or may use single formed lid in place of ring to cover inner lid. Do not tighten down too hard as it may impede sealing.
11. Place on protected surface to cool, taking care to not disturb lid and ring. A slight indentation of lid will be apparent when sealed.
12. When cooled, wipe jar with damp cloth then label and date each.
13. Leave overnight until thoroughly cooled and then they may be placed upright on shelf for storage.

Chocolate-Maple Breakfast
Syrup-in-a-Jar

I love my chocolate; but until this simple mix came along, I drew the line when it came to chocolate pancake syrup. This is the syrup that changed my mind!

Ingredients

½   c. chocolate syrup
½   c. maple-flavored pancake syrup

Directions

1.   In small bowl, combine chocolate syrup and pancake syrup.
2.   Pour into 1-cup glass jar.

Directions for Tag

1.   Serve Chocolate-Maple Breakfast Syrup with pancakes, waffles or French toast.
2.   Refrigerate leftover syrup.

Yields: 8 servings

Cranberry Jelly-in-a-Jar

This makes a great red jelly for the holidays. Place in decorative jars and it makes a great gift!

Ingredients:

2	c. cranberries
1	c. concentrated apple juice
¼	c. lemon juice
3	oz. liquid pectin (regular)
5	Tbs. glycerin
1	Tbs. unflavored gelatin

Directions:

1. Wash and pick over cranberries, discarding any that are soft.
2. Place in a deep saucepan and add fruit juices.
3. Cover and simmer for about 20 minutes, until fruit is soft.
4. Mash to break up any berries left whole.
5. Strain in food mill to remove seeds.
6. Return to saucepan and heat to boiling.
7. Add pectin, glycerin, and gelatin, stirring well.
8. Boil 1 minute; remove from heat.
9. Skim and pour into hot, sterile pint jars, leaving ½- inch at top.
10. Cap with hot sterile lids.
11. Process in boiling water bath for 5 minutes after water returns to boiling.
12. Note: If any jars fail to seal, refrigerate and use within 10 days or freeze for later use.

Yields: 3½ cups.

Hot Fudge Topping-in-a-Jar

This is absolutely THE hot fudge dream come true for a genuine chocolate lover! It's quick, it's easy, and it can adjust to your individual taste by adding a smidge more or less cocoa.

Ingredients:

2	c. sugar
½	c. cocoa
½	c. milk
½	c. butter
1	Tbs. corn syrup
	dash of salt

Directions:

1. In medium saucepan, mix all ingredients together.
2. Boil exactly 2 minutes and remove from heat. Do not boil longer as syrup will sugar.
3. Place in glass canning jar and twist on lid while still hot.

Directions for Tag

1. Serve this Hot Fudge Topping over ice cream.
2. May be served warm or cold; but be sure to remove metal lid if warming in microwave.
3. For leftover topping, stir in 1 tablespoon milk before placing in refrigerator.

Yields: 1 chocolate fix.

Mint Jelly-in-a-Jar

Mint is such a soothing flavor. Everyone will enjoy this traditional mint jelly made with fresh mint.

Ingredients:

1	c. of mint leaves, washed, then dried on paper towels
4	c. apple juice
4	c. white sugar
1	box powdered pectin (1.75 oz.)

5 or 6 drops green food coloring, optional

Directions:

1. In large saucepan, combine mint leaves, apple juice, food coloring, and pectin.
2. Bring to boil stirring in sugar until dissolved. Boil two minutes, remove from heat and skim off foam.
3. Pour into sterile jars, leaving ⅛-inch headspace. Wipe jar rims, adjust lids and rings. If desired, process in a hot water bath five minutes.
4. Note: You can finely chop the mint leaves and leave them in jelly, or wrap whole leaves in cheesecloth bag and remove before packing jelly in jars.

Direction for Tag

1. Use right out of the jar.

Sparkling Holiday Jam-in-a-Jar

This makes a great holiday red jam full of flavor and texture. It is also just beautiful to look at in a Jar!

Ingredients:

2½   qt. strawberries, coarsely chopped
1   pkg. fresh or frozen cranberries, chopped (12 oz.)
2   pkg. powdered fruit pectin (2 oz.)
1   tsp. butter
5   lb. white sugar

Directions:

1. Sterilize jars and lids in boiling water for at least 10 minutes.
2. Let simmer while making jam.
3. In large saucepan, combine strawberries, cranberries, pectin, and butter.
4. Bring to a boil; stir in sugar; return to boil.
5. Cook 1 minute; remove from heat.
6. Quickly fill jars to within ½-inch from top.
7. Wipe rims clean and put on lids.
8. Invert jars for 15 minutes to help them seal.

Spiced Pumpkin Pecan Butter-in-a-Jar

This is a wonderful jam with the holiday flavors of pumpkin and pecans.

Ingredients:

3½	c. canned pumpkin
1	c. pecans, toasted, chopped
1	Tbs. pumpkin pie spice
4½	c. sugar
1	box dry pectin (2 oz.)
½	tsp. butter

Directions:

1. In 6 to 8-quart saucepan, measure pumpkin, pecans, and pumpkin pie spice.
2. Prepare jars. Keep lids hot until ready to fill.
3. Measure sugar into separate bowl.
4. Stir fruit pectin into pumpkin mixture in saucepan.
5. Add butter; bring mixture to full rolling boil on high heat, stirring constantly.
6. Quickly stir in all sugar. Return to full rolling boil, and boil exactly 1 minute, stirring constantly.
7. Remove from heat; skim off any foam with metal spoon.
8. Ladle quickly into prepared jars, filling to within ¼-inch of tops.
9. Wipe jar rims and threads; cover with lids.
10. Screw on bands. Process in a water bath canner (180 to 190 degrees F.) for 15 minutes.
11. After jars are cool, check seals.

Yield: 5 half-pint jars.

My Notes

Notes

Notes

Notes

Notes

Notes

Notes

Notes

Notes

Notes

Acknowledgements

The author would like to acknowledge all those individuals who helped me during my time in writing this book. Appreciation is extended for all their support and effort they put into this project.

Deep gratitude and profound thanks are owed to my husband, Jim, for giving freely of his time and encouragement during this project.

Thanks are also owed to my children Gabriel, Brianne Kristina and her husband Moulik Vinodkumar Kothari, Marissa Kimberly and her husband Kevin Matthew Franck, Janelle Karina and her husband Paul Joseph Turcotte, Mikayla Karlene, Kyler James, Kelsey Katrina, Corbin Joel, Caleb Jerome, Keisha Kalani Hiwot, Devontay Joshua, Kianna Karielle Selam, Rosy Kiara, Mercedes Katherine, Jasmine Khalia Wengel, Cheyenne Krystal, and Annalise Kaylee Marie. All of these persons inspired my writing.

Thanks are due to Pam Alexandrovich and Sharron Thompson for their assistance in typing and editing this manuscript for publication. Thanks go to Artistic Design Service, Inc. for their assistance in formatting and providing a graphic design of this manuscript for publication. This project could not have been completed without them.

Many thanks are due to members of my family, all of whom were extremely supportive during the time it took to complete this project. Their patience and support are greatly appreciated.

Current and Future Cookbooks
By Karen Jean Matsko Hood

DELIGHTS SERIES
Almond Delights
Anchovy Delights
Apple Delights
Apricot Delights
Artichoke Delights
Asparagus Delights
Avocado Delights
Banana Delights
Barley Delights
Basil Delights
Bean Delights
Beef Delights
Beer Delights
Beet Delights
Blackberry Delights
Blueberry Delights
Bok Choy Delights
Boysenberry Delights
Brazil Nut Delights
Broccoli Delights
Brussels Sprouts Delights
Buffalo Berry Delights
Butter Delights
Buttermilk Delights
Cabbage Delights
Calamari Delights
Cantaloupe Delights
Caper Delights
Cardamom Delights
Carrot Delights
Cashew Delights
Cauliflower Delights
Celery Delights
Cheese Delights
Cherry Delights
Chestnut Delights
Chicken Delights

Chili Pepper Delights
Chive Delights
Chocolate Delights
Chokecherry Delights
Cilantro Delights
Cinnamon Delights
Clam Delights
Clementine Delights
Coconut Delights
Coffee Delights
Conch Delights
Corn Delights
Cottage Cheese Delights
Crab Delights
Cranberry Delights
Cucumber Delights
Cumin Delights
Curry Delights
Date Delights
Edamame Delights
Egg Delights
Eggplant Delights
Elderberry Delights
Endive Delights
Fennel Delights
Fig Delights
Filbert (Hazelnut) Delights
Fish Delights
Garlic Delights
Ginger Delights
Ginseng Delights
Goji Berry Delights
Grape Delights
Grapefruit Delights
Grapple Delights
Guava Delights
Ham Delights
Hamburger Delights

Herb Delights
Herbal Tea Delights
Honey Delights
Honeyberry Delights
Honeydew Delights
Horseradish Delights
Huckleberry Delights
Jalapeño Delights
Jerusalem Artichoke Delights
Jicama Delights
Kale Delights
Kiwi Delights
Kohlrabi Delights
Lavender Delights
Leek Delights
Lemon Delights
Lentil Delights
Lettuce Delights
Lime Delights
Lingonberry Delights
Lobster Delights
Loganberry Delights
Macadamia Nut Delights
Mango Delights
Marionberry Delights
Milk Delights
Mint Delights
Miso Delights
Mushroom Delights
Mussel Delights
Nectarine Delights
Oatmeal Delights
Olive Delights
Onion Delights
Orange Delights
Oregon Berry Delights
Oyster Delights
Papaya Delights
Parsley Delights
Parsnip Delights

Pea Delights
Peach Delights
Peanut Delights
Pear Delights
Pecan Delights
Pepper Delights
Persimmon Delights
Pine Nut Delights
Pineapple Delights
Pistachio Delights
Plum Delights
Pomegranate Delights
Pomelo Delights
Popcorn Delights
Poppy Seed Delights
Pork Delights
Potato Delights
Prickly Pear Cactus Delights
Prune Delights
Pumpkin Delights
Quince Delights
Quinoa Delights
Radish Delights
Raisin Delights
Raspberry Delights
Rhubarb Delights
Rice Delights
Rose Delights
Rosemary Delights
Rutabaga Delights
Salmon Delights
Salmonberry Delights
Salsify Delights
Savory Delights
Scallop Delights
Seaweed Delights
Serviceberry Delights
Sesame Delights
Shallot Delights
Shrimp Delights

Soybean Delights
Spinach Delights
Squash Delights
Star Fruit Delights
Strawberry Delights
Sunflower Seed Delights
Sweet Potato Delights
Swiss Chard Delights
Tangerine Delights
Tapioca Delights
Tayberry Delights
Tea Delights
Teaberry Delights
Thimbleberry Delights
Tofu Delights
Tomatillo Delights
Tomato Delights
Trout Delights
Truffle Delights
Tuna Delights
Turkey Delights
Turmeric Delights
Turnip Delights
Vanilla Delights
Walnut Delights
Wasabi Delights
Watermelon Delights
Wheat Delights
Wild Rice Delights
Yam Delights
Yogurt Delights
Zucchini Delights

CITY DELIGHTS
Chicago Delights
Coeur d'Alene Delights
Great Falls Delights
Honolulu Delights
Minneapolis Delights
Phoenix Delights

Portland Delights
Sandpoint Delights
Scottsdale Delights
Seattle Delights
Spokane Delights
St. Cloud Delights

FOSTER CARE
Foster Children Cookbook
  and Activity Book
Foster Children's Favorite
  Recipes
Holiday Cookbook for
  Foster Families

GENERAL THEME DELIGHTS
Appetizer Delights
Baby Food Delights
Barbeque Delights
Beer-Making Delights
Beverage Delights
Biscotti Delights
Bisque Delights
Blender Delights
Bread Delights
Bread Maker Delights
Breakfast Delights
Brunch Delights
Cake Delights
Campfire Food Delights
Candy Delights
Canned Food Delights
Cast Iron Delights
Cheesecake Delights
Chili Delights
Chowder Delights
Cocktail Delights
College Cooking Delights
Comfort Food Delights

Cookie Delights
Cooking for One Delights
Cooking for Two Delights
Cracker Delights
Crepe Delights
Crockpot Delights
Dairy Delights
Dehydrated Food Delights
Dessert Delights
Dinner Delights
Dutch Oven Delights
Foil Delights
Fondue Delights
Food Processor Delights
Fried Food Delights
Frozen Food Delights
Fruit Delights
Gelatin Delights
Grilled Delights
Hiking Food Delights
Ice Cream Delights
Juice Delights
Kid's Delights
Kosher Diet Delights
Liqueur-Making Delights
Liqueurs and Spirits Delights
Lunch Delights
Marinade Delights
Microwave Delights
Milk Shake and Malt Delights
Panini Delights
Pasta Delights
Pesto Delights
Phyllo Delights
Pickled Food Delights
Picnic Food Delights
Pizza Delights
Preserved Delights
Pudding and Custard Delights
Quiche Delights

Quick Mix Delights
Rainbow Delights
Salad Delights
Salsa Delights
Sandwich Delights
Sea Vegetable Delights
Seafood Delights
Smoothie Delights
Snack Delights
Soup Delights
Supper Delights
Tart Delights
Torte Delights
Tropical Delights
Vegan Delights
Vegetable Delights
Vegetarian Delights
Vinegar Delights
Wildflower Delights
Wine Delights
Winemaking Delights
Wok Delights

GIFTS-IN-A-JAR COOKBOOK SERIES
Christmas Gifts-in-a-Jar –
   Book 1
Gifts-in-a-Jar – Book 2
Holiday Gifts-in-a-Jar –
   Book 3

HEALTH-RELATED DELIGHTS
Achalasia Diet Delights
Adrenal Health Diet Delights
Anti-Acid Reflux Diet Delights
Anti-Cancer Diet Delights
Anti-Inflammation Diet
   Delights
Anti-Stress Diet Delights

Arthritis Delights
Bone Health Diet Delights
Diabetic Diet Delights
Diet for Pink Delights
Fibromyalgia Diet Delights
Gluten-Free Diet Delights
Healthy Breath Diet Delights
Healthy Digestion Diet
  Delights
Healthy Heart Diet Delights
Healthy Skin Diet Delights
Healthy Teeth Diet Delights
High-Fiber Diet Delights
High-Iodine Diet Delights
High-Protein Diet Delights
Immune Health Diet Delights
Kidney Health Diet Delights
Lactose-Free Diet Delights
Liquid Diet Delights
Liver Health Diet Delights
Low-Calorie Diet Delights
Low-Carb Diet Delights
Low-Fat Diet Delights
Low-Sodium Diet Delights
Low-Sugar Diet Delights
Lymphoma Health Support
  Diet Delights
Multiple Sclerosis Healthy
  Diet Delights
No Flour No Sugar Diet
  Delights
Organic Food Delights
pH-Friendly Diet Delights
Pregnancy Diet Delights
Raw Food Diet Delights
Sjögren's Syndrome Diet
  Delights
Soft Food Diet Delights
Thyroid Health Diet Delights

HOLIDAY DELIGHTS
Christmas Delights
Easter Delights
Father's Day Delights
Fourth of July Delights
Grandparent's Day Delights
Halloween Delights
Hanukkah Delights
Labor Day Delights
Memorial Day Delights
Mother's Day Delights
New Year's Delights
St. Patrick's Day Delights
Thanksgiving Delights
Valentine Delights

**HOOD AND MATSKO
FAMILY FAVORITES**
Hood and Matsko Family
  Appetizers Cookbook
Hood and Matsko Family
  Beverages Cookbook
Hood and Matsko Family
  Breads and Rolls Cookbook
Hood and Matsko Family
  Breakfasts Cookbook
Hood and Matsko Family
  Cakes Cookbook
Hood and Matsko Family
  Candies Cookbook
Hood and Matsko Family
  Casseroles Cookbook
Hood and Matsko Family
  Cookies Cookbook
Hood and Matsko Family
  Desserts Cookbook
Hood and Matsko Family
  Dressings, Sauces, and
  Condiments Cookbook
Hood and Matsko Family

Ethnic Cookbook
Hood and Matsko Family
  Jams, Jellies, Syrups,
  Preserves, and Conserves
Hood and Matsko Family
  Main Dishes Cookbook
Hood and Matsko Family,
  Pies Cookbook
Hood and Matsko Family
  Preserving Cookbook
Hood and Matsko Family
  Salads and Salad Dressings
Hood and Matsko Family
  Side Dishes Cookbook
Hood and Matsko Family
  Vegetable Cookbook
Hood and Matsko Family,
  Aunt Katherine's Recipe
  Collection, Vol. I-II
Hood and Matsko Family,
  Grandma Bert's Recipe
  Collection, Books 1-8

HOOD AND MATSKO
FAMILY HOLIDAY
Hood and Matsko Family
  Favorite Birthday Recipes
Hood and Matsko Family
  Favorite Christmas Recipes
Hood and Matsko Family
  Favorite Christmas Sweets
Hood and Matsko Family
  Easter Cookbook
Hood and Matsko Family
  Favorite Thanksgiving Recipes

INTERNATIONAL
DELIGHTS
African Delights
African American Delights

Australian Delights
Austrian Delights
Brazilian Delights
Canadian Delights
Chilean Delights
Chinese Delights
Czechoslovakian Delights
English Delights
Ethiopian Delights
Fijian Delights
French Delights
German Delights
Greek Delights
Hungarian Delights
Icelandic Delights
Indian Delights
Irish Delights
Italian Delights
Korean Delights
Kosovo Delights
Macedonia Republic Delights
Mexican Delights
Montenegro Delights
Native American Delights
Polish Delights
Russian Delights
Scottish Delights
Serbian Delights
Slovakian Delights
Slovenian Delights
Sri Lanka Delights
Swedish Delights
Thai Delights
The Netherlands Delights
Yugoslavian Delights
Zambian Delights

REGIONAL DELIGHTS
Glacier National Park Delights
Northwest Regional Delights

Oregon Coast Delights
Schweitzer Mountain Delights
Southwest Regional Delights
Tropical Delights
Washington Wine Country
    Delights
Wine Delights of Walla
    Walla Wineries
Yellowstone National Park
    Delights

SEASONAL DELIGHTS
Autumn Harvest Delights
Spring Harvest Delights
Summer Harvest Delights
Winter Harvest Delights

SPECIAL EVENTS
DELIGHTS
Birthday Delights
Coffee Klatch Delights
Super Bowl Delights
Tea Time Delights

STATE DELIGHTS
Alaska Delights
Arizona Delights
Georgia Delights
Hawaii Delights
Idaho Delights
Illinois Delights
Iowa Delights
Louisiana Delights
Minnesota Delights
Montana Delights
North Dakota Delights
Oregon Delights
South Dakota Delights
Texas Delights
Washington Delights

U.S. TERRITORIES
DELIGHTS
Cruzan Delights
U.S. Virgin Island Delights

MISCELLANEOUS
COOKBOOKS
Getaway Studio Cookbook
The Soup Doctor's Cookbook

BILINGUAL DELIGHTS
SERIES
Apple Delights, English-
    French Edition
Apple Delights, English-
    Russian Edition
Apple Delights, English-
    Spanish Edition
Huckleberry Delights,
    English-French Edition
Huckleberry Delights,
    English-Russian Edition
Huckleberry Delights,
    English-Spanish Edition

CATHOLIC DELIGHTS
SERIES
Apple Delights Catholic
Coffee Delights Catholic
Easter Delights Catholic
Huckleberry Delights Catholic
Tea Delights Catholic

CATHOLIC BILINGUAL
DELIGHTS SERIES
Apple Delights Catholic,
    English-French Edition
Apple Delights Catholic,
    English-Russian Edition
Apple Delights Catholic,

English-Spanish Edition
Huckleberry Delights
  Catholic, English-Spanish
  Edition

CHRISTIAN DELIGHTS SERIES

Apple Delights Christian
Coffee Delights Christian
Easter Delights Christian
Huckleberry Delights Christian
Tea Delights Christian

CHRISTIAN BILINGUAL DELIGHTS SERIES

Apple Delights Christian,
  English-French Edition
Apple Delights Christian,
  English-Russian Edition
Apple Delights Christian,
  English-Spanish Edition
Huckleberry Delights
  Christian, English-Spanish
  Edition

FUNDRAISING COOKBOOKS

Ask about our fundraising
  cookbooks to help raise
  funds for your organization.

The above books are also available in bilingual versions. Please contact Whispering Pine Press International, Inc., for details.

The above list of books is not all-inclusive. For a complete list please visit our website or contact us at:

Whispering Pine Press International, Inc.
Your Northwest Book Publishing Company
2510 North Pines Road, Suite 206, Sales Room
Spokane Valley, WA 99206-7636 USA
Phone: (509) 928-7888 | Fax: (509) 922-9949
Email: sales@whisperingpinepress.com
Publisher Websites: www.WhisperingPinePress.com www.
WhisperingPinePressBookstore.com
Blog: www.WhisperingPinePressBlog.com

Publisher Websites:
Main Website: WhisperingPinePress.com
Online Store: WhisperingPinePressBookstore.com
WordPress Blogs: WhisperingPinePressBlog.com
WhisperingPinePressKidsBooks.com
WhisperingPinePressTeenBooks.com
WhisperingPinePressPoetry.com

Karen Jean Matsko Hood
Author Website: KarenJeanMatskoHood.com
Online Store: KarenJeanMatskoHoodBookstore.com
Author Blog: KarenJeanMatskoHoodBlog.com
Kids Books: KarensKidsBooks.com
Teen Books: KarensTeenBooks.com

Author's Social Media
Like or Friend the Author on Facebook:
https://www.facebook.com/KarenJeanMatskoHoodAuthor
FanPage
Follow the Author on Twitter: https://twitter.com/KarenJeanHood
Google Plus Profile: http://google.com/+KarenJeanMatskoHood

Glossary

Aerate: A synonym for sift; to pass ingredients through a fine-mesh device to break up large pieces and incorporate air into ingredients to make them lighter.

Al dente: "To the tooth," in Italian. The pasta is cooked just enough to maintain a firm, chewy texture.

Baste: To brush or spoon liquid fat or juices over meat during roasting to add flavor and prevent it from drying out.

Bias-slice: To slice a food crosswise at a 45-degree angle.

Bind: To thicken a sauce or hot liquid by stirring in ingredients such as eggs, flour, butter, or cream.

Blackened: Popular Cajun-style cooking method. Seasoned foods are cooked over high heat in a super-heated heavy skillet until charred.

Blanch: To boil briefly to loosen the skin of a fruit or a vegetable. After 30 seconds in boiling water, the fruit or vegetable should be plunged into ice water to stop the cooking action, and then the skin easily peels off.

Blend: To mix or fold two or more ingredients together to obtain equal distribution throughout the mixture.

Braise: A cooking technique that requires browning meat in oil or other fat and then cooking slowly in liquid. The effect of braising is to tenderize the meat.

Bread: To coat the food with crumbs (usually with soft or dry bread crumbs), sometimes seasoned.

Brown: A quick sautéing, pan/oven broiling, or grilling method done either at the beginning or end of meal preparation, often to enhance flavor, texture, or eye appeal.

Brush: Using a pastry brush, to coat a food such as meat or bread with melted butter, glaze, or other liquid.

Bundt pan: The generic name for any tube baking pan having fluted sides (though it was once a trademarked name).

Butterfly: To cut open a food such as pork chops down the center without cutting all the way through, and then spread apart.

Caramelization: Browning sugar over a flame, with or without the addition of some water to aid the process. The temperature range in which sugar caramelizes is approximately 320° F to 360° F (160° C to 182° C).

Clarify: Remove impurities from butter or stock by heating the liquid, then straining or skimming it.

Coddle: A cooking method in which foods (such as eggs) are put in separate containers and placed in a pan of simmering water for slow, gentle cooking.

Confit: To slowly cook pieces of meat in their own gently rendered fat.

Core: To remove the inedible center of fruits such as pineapples.

Cream: To beat vegetable shortening, butter, or margarine, with or without sugar, until light and fluffy. This process traps in air bubbles, later used to create height in cookies and cakes.

Crimp: To create a decorative edge on a piecrust. On a double piecrust, this also seals the edges together.

Curd: Custard-like pie or tart filling flavored with juice and zest of citrus fruit, usually lemon, although lime and orange may also be used.

Curdle: To cause semisolid pieces of coagulated protein to develop in food, usually as a result of the addition of an acid substance, or the overheating of milk or egg-based sauces.

Custard: A mixture of beaten egg, milk, and possibly other ingredients such as sweet or savory flavorings, which is cooked with gentle heat, often in a water bath or double boiler. As pie filling, the custard is frequently cooked and chilled before being layered into a baked crust.

Deglaze: To add liquid to a pan in which foods have been fried or roasted, in order to dissolve the caramelized juices stuck to the bottom of the pan.

Dot: To sprinkle food with small bits of an ingredient such as butter to allow for even melting.

Dredge: To sprinkle lightly and evenly with sugar or flour. A dredger has holes pierced on the lid to sprinkle evenly.

Drizzle: To pour a liquid such as a sweet glaze or melted butter in a slow, light trickle over food.

Drippings: Used for gravies and sauces, drippings are the liquids left in the bottom of a roasting or frying pan after meat is cooked.

Dust: To sprinkle food lightly with spices, sugar, or flour for a light coating.

Egg wash: A mixture of beaten eggs (yolks, whites, or whole eggs) with either milk or water. Used to coat cookies and other baked goods to give them a shine when baked.

Emulsion: A mixture of liquids, one being a fat or oil and the other being water based so that tiny globules of one are suspended in the other. This may involve the use of stabilizers, such as egg or mustard. Emulsions may be temporary or permanent.

Entrée: A French term that originally referred to the first course of a meal, served after the soup and before the meat courses. In the United States, it refers to the main dish of a meal.

Fillet: To remove the bones from meat or fish for cooking.

Filter: To remove lumps, excess liquid, or impurities by passing through paper or cheesecloth.

Firm-ball stage: In candy making, the point where boiling syrup dropped in cold water forms a ball that is compact yet gives slightly to the touch.

Flambé: To ignite a sauce or other liquid so that it flames.

Flan: An open pie filled with sweet or savory ingredients; also, a Spanish dessert of baked custard covered with caramel.

Flute: To create a decorative scalloped or undulating edge on a piecrust or other pastry.

Fricassee: Usually a stew in which the meat is cut up, lightly cooked in butter, and then simmered in liquid until done.

Frizzle: To cook thin slices of meat in hot oil until crisp and slightly curly.

Ganache: A rich chocolate filling or coating made with chocolate, vegetable shortening, and possibly heavy cream. It can coat cakes or cookies, and be used as a filling for truffles.

Glaze: A liquid that gives an item a shiny surface. Examples are fruit jams that have been heated or chocolate thinned with melted vegetable shortening. Also, to cover a food with such a liquid.

Gratin: To bind together or combine food with a liquid such as cream, milk, béchamel sauce, or tomato sauce, in a shallow dish. The mixture is then baked until cooked and set.

Hard-ball stage: In candy making, the point at which syrup has cooked long enough to form a solid ball in cold water.

Hull (also husk): To remove the leafy parts of soft fruits, such as strawberries or blackberries.

Infusion: Extracting flavors by soaking them in liquid heated in a covered pan. The term also refers to the liquid resulting from this process.

Jerk or Jamaican jerk seasoning: A dry mixture of various spices such as chilies, thyme, garlic, onions, and cinnamon or cloves used to season meats such as chicken or pork.

Julienne: To cut into long, thin strips.

Jus: The natural juices released by roasting meats.

Larding: Inserting strips of fat into pieces of meat, so that the braised meat stays moist and juicy.

Marble: To gently swirl one food into another.

Marinate: To combine food with aromatic ingredients to add flavor.

Meringue: Egg whites beaten until they are stiff, then sweetened. It can be used as the topping for pies, or baked as cookies.

Mull: To slowly heat wine or cider with spices and sugar.

Parboil: To partly cook in a boiling liquid.

Peaks: The mounds made in a mixture. For example, egg white that has been whipped to stiffness. Peaks are "stiff" if they stay upright, or "soft" if they curl over.

Pesto: A sauce usually made of fresh basil, garlic, olive oil, pine nuts, and cheese. The ingredients are finely chopped and then mixed, uncooked, with pasta. Generally, the term refers to any uncooked sauce made of finely chopped herbs and nuts.

Pipe: To force a semi-soft food through a bag (either a pastry bag or a plastic bag with one corner cut off) to decorate food.

Pressure Cooking: A cooking method that uses steam trapped under a locked lid to produce high temperatures and achieve fast cooking time.

Ramekin: A small baking dish used for individual servings of sweet and savory dishes.

Reduce: To cook liquids down so that some of the water evaporates.

Refresh: To pour cold water over freshly cooked vegetables to prevent further cooking and to retain color.

Roux: A cooked paste usually made from flour and butter used to thicken sauces.

Sauté: To cook food quickly in a small amount of oil in a skillet or sauté pan over direct heat.

Sear: Sealing in a meat's juices by cooking it quickly under very high heat.

Seize: To form a thick, lumpy mass when melted (usually applied to chocolate).

Sift: To remove large lumps from a dry ingredient such as flour or confectioners' sugar by passing it through a fine mesh. This process also incorporates air into the ingredients, making them lighter.

Simmer: Cooking food in a liquid at a low enough temperature that small bubbles begin to break the surface.

Steam: To cook over boiling water in a covered pan, this method keeps foods' shape, texture, and nutritional value intact better than methods such as boiling.

Steep: To soak dry ingredients (tea leaves, ground coffee, herbs, spices, etc.) in liquid until the flavor is infused into the liquid.

Stewing: Browning small pieces of meat, poultry, or fish, then simmering them with vegetables or other ingredients in enough liquid to cover them, usually in a closed pot on the stove, in the oven, or with a slow cooker.

Thin: To reduce a mixture's thickness with the addition of more liquid.

Truss: To use string, skewers, or pins to hold together a food to maintain its shape while it cooks (usually applied to meat or poultry).

Unleavened: Baked goods that contain no agents to give them volume, such as baking powder, baking soda, or yeast.

Vinaigrette: A general term referring to any sauce made with vinegar, oil, and seasonings.

Zest: The thin, brightly colored outer part of the rind of citrus fruits. It contains volatile oils, used as a flavoring.

U.S. and Metric Measurement Charts

Here are some measurement equivalents to help you with exchanges. There was a time when many people thought the entire world would convert to the metric scale. While most of the world has, America still has not. Metric conversions in cooking are vitally important to preparing a tasty recipe. Here are simple conversion tables that should come in handy.

U.S. Measurement Equivalents

a few grains/pinch/dash (dry) = less than ⅛ teaspoon
a dash (liquid) = a few drops
3 teaspoons = 1 tablespoon
½ tablespoon = 1½ teaspoons
1 tablespoon = 3 teaspoons
2 tablespoons = 1 fluid ounce
4 tablespoons = ¼ cup
5⅓ tablespoons = ⅓ cup
8 tablespoons = ½ cup
8 tablespoons = 4 fluid ounces
10⅔ tablespoons = ⅔ cup
12 tablespoons = ¾ cup
16 tablespoons = 1 cup
16 tablespoons = 8 fluid ounces
⅛ cup = 2 tablespoons
¼ cup = 4 tablespoons
¼ cup = 2 fluid ounces
⅓ cup = 5 tablespoons plus 1 teaspoon
½ cup = 8 tablespoons
1 cup = 16 tablespoons
1 cup = 8 fluid ounces
1 cup = ½ pint
2 cups = 1 pint
2 pints = 1 quart
4 quarts (liquid) = 1 gallon
8 quarts (dry) = 1 peck
4 pecks (dry) = 1 bushel
1 kilogram = approximately 2 pounds
1 liter=approximately 4 cups or 1quart

Approximate Metric Equivalents by Volume

U.S.	Metric
¼ cup	= 60 milliliters
½ cup	= 120 milliliters
1 cup	= 230 milliliters
1¼ cups	= 300 milliliters
1½ cups	= 360 milliliters
2 cups	= 460 milliliters
2½ cups	= 600 milliliters
3 cups	= 700 milliliters
4 cups (1 quart)	= .95 liter
1.06 quarts	= 1 liter
4 quarts (1 gallon)	= 3.8 liters

Approximate Metric Equivalents by Weight

U.S.	Metric
¼ ounce	= 7 grams
½ ounce	= 14 grams
1 ounce	= 28 grams
1¼ ounces	= 35 grams
1½ ounces	= 40 grams
2½ ounces	= 70 grams
4 ounces	= 112 grams
5 ounces	= 140 grams
8 ounces	= 228 grams
10 ounces	= 280 grams
15 ounces	= 425 grams
16 ounces (1 pound)	= 454 grams

Christmas Gifts-in-a-Jar Cookbook Index

Breads and Muffins

Breakfast

Cakes

Candies

Cookies

Dressings, Sauces, and Condiments

Jams, Jellies, and Syrups

Reader Feedback Form

Dear Reader,

We are very interested in what our readers think. Please fill in the form below and return to:

Whispering Pine Press International, Inc.
International Publishing Company
c/o Christmas Gifts-in-a-Jar Cookbook
2510 North Pines Road, Suite 206, Sales Room
Spokane Valley, WA 99206-7636 USA
Phone: (509) 928-7888 | Fax: (509) 922-9949
Email: sales@whisperingpinepress.com
Website: www.WhisperingPinePress.com
www.WhisperingPinePressBookstore.com
Blog: www.WhisperingPinePressBlog.com
SANS #253-200X

Name: _____

Address: _____

City, St., Zip: _____

Phone/Fax: (____) _____ | (____) _____

Email: _____

Comments/Suggestions: _____

_____

_____

_____

_____

A great deal of care and attention has been exercised in the creation of this book. Designing a great cookbook that is original, fun, and easy to use has been a job that required many hours of diligence, creativity, and research. Although we strive to make this book completely error free, errors and discrepancies may not be completely excluded. If you come across any errors or discrepancies, please make a note of them and send them to our publishing office. We are constantly updating our manuscripts, eliminating errors, and improving quality.

Please contact us at the address above.

About the Gifts-in-a-Jar Series

The *Gifts-in-a-Jar Cookbook Series* includes many different recipes that are fun and easy to make. If you have a passion for food and wish to make some great gifts to share with friends and family, then this series of cookbooks will be beneficial to you.

Gifts-in-a-Jar Cookbook Series includes Christmas Gifts-in-a-Jar, Gifts-in-a-Jar and Holiday Gifts-in-a-Jar. Each book features different types of recipes for Gifts-in-a-Jar.

Whatever your favorite holiday may be, chances are we have a cookbook with recipes designed with that holiday in mind. Some examples include *Valentine Delights, St. Patrick's Day Delights, Easter Delights, Mother's Day Delights, Halloween Delights, Thanksgiving Delights, and Christmas Delights.*

Each cookbook is designed for easy use and is organized into alphabetical sections. Each book comes with a beautiful full-color cover, ordering information, and a list of other upcoming books in the series.

Note cards, bookmarks, and a daily journal have been printed and are available to go along with each cookbook. You may view the entire line of cookbooks, journals, cards, posters, puzzles, and bookmarks by visiting our website at www.WhisperingPinePressBookstore.com, or you can email us with your questions and your comments to: sales@whisperingpinepress.com.

Please ask your local bookstore to carry these sets of books.

To order, please contact:

Whispering Pine Press International, Inc.
International Publishing Company
c/o Christmas Gifts-in-a-Jar Cookbook
2510 North Pines Road, Suite 206, Sales Room
Spokane Valley, WA 99206-7636
Phone: (509) 928-7888 | Fax: (509) 922-9949
Email: sales@whisperingpinepress.com
Publisher Websites: www.WhisperingPinePress.com
www.WhisperingPinePressBookstore.com
Blog: www.WhisperingPinePressBlog.com
SAN 253-200X

We Invite You to Join the
Whispering Pine Press International, Inc.
Loyalty Book Club!

Whispering Pine Press International, Inc.
International Publishing Company
c/o Christmas Gifts-in-a-Jar Cookbook
2510 North Pines Road, Suite 206, Sales Room
Spokane Valley, WA 99206-7636
Phone: (509) 928-7888 | Fax: (509) 922-9949
Email: sales@whisperingpinepress.com
Publisher Websites: www.WhisperingPinePress.com
www.WhisperingPinePressBookstore.com
Blog: www.WhisperingPinePressBlog.com

Buy 11 books and get the next one free, based on the average price of the first eleven purchased. This is your reward for your loyalty to our company.

How the club works:

Simply use the order form below and order books from our catalog. You can buy just one at a time or all eleven at once. After the first eleven books are purchased, the next one is free. Please add shipping and handling as listed on this form. There are no purchase requirements at any time during your membership. Free book credit is based on the average price of the first eleven books purchased.

Join today! Pick your books and mail in the form today!

Yes! I want to join the Whispering Pine Press International, Inc., Book Club! Enroll me and send the books indicated below.

<u>Title</u>   <u>Price</u>

1. _____
2. _____
3. _____
4. _____
5. _____
6. _____
7. _____
8. _____
9. _____
10. _____
11. _____

Free Book Title: _____

Free Book Price: _____Avg. Price: _____ Total Price: _____

Credit for the free book is based on the average price of the first 11 books purchased.

(Circle one) Check | Visa | MasterCard | Discover | American Express

Credit Card #: _____ Expiration Date: _____

Name: _____

Address: _____

City: _____State: _____Country: _____

Zip/Postal: _____Phone: (_____) _____

Email: _____

        Signature_____

Whispering Pine Press International, Inc.
Fundraising Opportunities

Fundraising cookbooks are proven moneymakers and great keepsake providers for your group. Whispering Pine Press International, Inc., offers a very special personalized cookbook fundraising program that encourages success to organizations all across the USA.

Our prices are competitive and fair. Currently, we offer a special of 100 books with many free features and excellent customer service. Any purchase you make is guaranteed first-rate.

Flexibility is not a problem. If you have special needs, we guarantee our cooperation in meeting each of them. Our goal is to create a cookbook that goes beyond your expectations. We have the confidence and a record that promises continual success.

Another great fundraising program is the *Cookbook Delights Series* Program. With cookbook orders of 50 copies or more, your organization receives a huge discount, making for a prompt and lucrative solution.

We also specialize in assisting group fundraising – Christian, community, nonprofit, and academic among them. If you are struggling for a new idea, something that will enhance your success and broaden your appeal, Whispering Pine Press International, Inc., can help.

For more information, write, phone, or fax to:

Whispering Pine Press International, Inc.
International Publishing Company
2510 North Pines Road, Suite 206, Sales Room
Spokane Valley, WA 99206-7636
Phone: (509) 928-7888 | Fax: (509) 922-9949
Email: sales@whisperingpinepress.com
Publisher Websites: www.WhisperingPinePress.com
www.WhisperingPinePressBookstore.com
Blog: www.WhisperingPinePressBlog.com
SAN 253-200X

Personalized and/or Translated
Order Form for Any Book by
Whispering Pine Press International, Inc.

Dear Readers:

If you or your organization wishes to have this book or any other of our books personalized, we will gladly accommodate your needs. For instance, if you would like to change the names of the characters in a book to the names of the children in your family or Sunday school class, we would be happy to work with you on such a project. We can add more information of your choosing and customize this book especially for your family, group, or organization.

We are also offering an option of translating your book into another language. Please fill out the form below telling us exactly how you would like us to personalize your book.

Please send your request to:

Whispering Pine Press International, Inc.
International Publishing Company
c/o Christmas Gifts-in-a-Jar Cookbook
2510 North Pines Road, Suite 206, Sales Room
Spokane Valley, WA 99206-7636
Phone: (509) 928-7888 | Fax: (509) 922-9949
Email: sales@whisperingpinepress.com
Publisher Websites: www.WhisperingPinePress.com
www.WhisperingPinePressBookstore.com
Blog: www.WhisperingPinePressBlog.com

Person/Organization placing request: _____

Date_____ Phone: (____)_____

Address_____ Fax: (____)_____

City_____ State_____ Zip: _____

Language of the book: _____

Please explain your request in detail: _____

_____

_____

_____

_____

_____

Christmas Gifts-in-a-Jar Cookbook
A Collection of Christmas Gifts-in-a-Jar Recipes
How to Order

Get your additional copies of this book by returning an order form and your check, money order, or credit card information to:

Whispering Pine Press International, Inc.
International Publishing Company
c/o Christmas Gifts-in-a-Jar Cookbook
2510 North Pines Road, Suite 206, Sales Room
Spokane Valley, WA 99206-7636
Phone: (509) 928-7888 | Fax: (509) 922-9949
Email: sales@whisperingpinepress.com
Publisher Websites: www.WhisperingPinePress.com
www.WhisperingPinePressBookstore.com
Blog: www.WhisperingPinePressBlog.com

Customer Name: _____

Address: _____

City, St., Zip: _____

Phone/Fax: _____

Email: _____

- -

Please send me _____ copies of _____

_____ at $_____ per copy and $5.95 for shipping and handling per book, plus $3.95 each for additional books. Enclosed is my check, money order, or charge my account for $_____.

☐ Check   ☐ Money Order   ☐ Credit Card

(*Circle One*) MasterCard | Discover | Visa | American Express

☐☐☐☐   ☐☐☐☐   ☐☐☐☐   ☐☐☐☐

Expiration Date: _____

_____
Signature
_____

Whispering Pine Press International, Inc. Order Form

Gift-wrapping, Autographing, and Inscription

We are proud to offer personal autographing by the author. For a limited time this service is absolutely free! Gift-wrapping is also available for $4.95 per item.

1. Sold To

Name: _____
Street/Route: _____
_____
City: _____
State: _____ Zip: _____
Country: _____
Gift message: _____
_____
Email address: _____
Daytime Phone: (_ _) _ _ _-_ _ _ _
*Necessary for verifying orders
Home Phone: (_ _) _ _ _-_ _ _ _
Fax: (_ _) _ _ _-_ _ _ _

2. Ship To

☐ Is this a new or corrected address?

☐ Alternative Shipping Address

☐ Mailing Address

Name: _____
Address: _____
_____
City: _____
State: _____ Zip: _____
Country: _____
Email address: _____

3. Items Ordered

ISBN # /Item #	Size	Color	Qty.	Title or Description	Price	Total

4. Method Of Payment

International, Inc. (No Cash or COD's)

☐ Visa ☐ MasterCard ☐ Discover ☐ American Express ☐ Check/Money Order

Please make it payable to Whispering Pine Press International, Inc. (No Cash or COD's)

Account Number   Expiration Date
                                  _____ /_____
                                  Month Year

☐☐☐☐☐☐☐☐☐☐☐☐☐☐☐☐☐☐

Signature_____
Cardholder's signature

Printed Name_____
Please print name of cardholder

Address of Cardholder_____

Subtotal	
Gift wrap $4.95 Each	
For delivery in WA add 8.7% sales tax.	
Shipping See chart at left	
6. Total	

5. Shipping & Handling

Continental US

US Postal Ground: For books please add $4.95 for the first book and $2.95 each for additional books.
All non-book items, add 15% of the Subtotal.
Please allow 1-4 weeks for delivery.
US Postal Air: Please add $15.00 shipping and handling.
Please allow 1-3 days for delivery.
Alaska, Hawaii, and the US Territories By Ship:
Please add 10% shipping and handling
(minimum charge $15.00).

Please
By Air: Please add 12% shipping and handling (minimum charge $15.00).
Please allow 2 –6 weeks for delivery.
International By Ship: Please add 10% shipping and handling (minimum charge $15.00).
Please allow 6-12 weeks for delivery.
By Air: Please add 12% shipping and handling (minimum charge $15.00).
Please allow 2-6 weeks for delivery.
FedEx Shipments: Add $5.00 to the above airmail charges for overnight delivery.

Shop Online:
www.WhisperingPinePress.com
Fax orders to: (509) 922-9949

Whispering Pine Press International, Inc.
2510 North Pines Road, Suite 206, Sales Room
Spokane Valley, WA 99206-7636 USA
Phone: (509) 928-7888 • Fax: (509) 922-9949
Email: sales@whisperingpinepress.com
Website: www.WhisperingPinePress.com

About the Author and Cook

Karen Jean Matsko Hood has always enjoyed cooking, baking, and experimenting with recipes. At this time Hood is working to complete a series of cookbooks that blends her skills and experience in cooking and entertaining. Hood entertains large groups of people and especially enjoys designing creative menus with holiday, international, ethnic, and regional themes.

Hood is publishing a cookbook series entitled the *Cookbook Delights Series*, in which each cookbook emphasizes a different food ingredient or theme. The first cookbook in the series is *Apple Delights Cookbook*. Hood is working to complete another series of cookbooks titled *Hood and Matsko Family Cookbooks*, which includes many recipes handed down from her family heritage and others that have emerged from more current family traditions. She has been invited to speak on talk radio shows on various topics, and favorite recipes from her cookbooks have been prepared on local television programs.

Hood was born and raised in Great Falls, Montana. As an undergraduate, she attended the College of St. Benedict in St. Joseph, Minnesota, and St. John's University in Collegeville, Minnesota. She attended the University of Great Falls in Great Falls, Montana. Hood received a B.S. Degree in Natural Science from the College of St. Benedict and minored in both Psychology and Secondary Education. Upon her graduation, Hood and her husband taught science and math on the island of St. Croix in the U.S. Virgin Islands. Hood has completed postgraduate classes at the University of Iowa in Iowa City, Iowa. In May 2001, she completed her Master's Degree in Pastoral Ministry at Gonzaga University in Spokane, Washington. She has taken postgraduate classes at Lewis and Clark College on the North Idaho college campus in Coeur d'Alene, Idaho, Taylor University in Fort Wayne, Indiana, Spokane Falls Community College, Spokane Community College, Washington State University, University of Washington, and Eastern Washington University. Hood is working on research projects to complete her Ph.D. in Leadership Studies at Gonzaga University in Spokane, Washington.

Karen Hood resides in Spokane, Washington, along with her husband, and many of her sixteen children, and foster children. Her interests include writing, research, and teaching. She previously has volunteered as a court advocate in the Spokane juvenile court system for abused and neglected children. Being a literary advocate for youth and adults, her hobbies include cooking, baking, collecting, photography, indoor and outdoor gardening, farming, and the cultivation of unusual flowering plants and orchids. She enjoys raising several specialty breeds of animals including Babydoll Southdown, Friesen, and Icelandic sheep, Icelandic and Arabian horses, Shetland pony, a variety of

Nubian and fainting goats, many breeds of chickens, ducks, geese, and other poultry, a few rescue cats, bichons frisés, cockapoos, Icelandic sheepdogs, a Newfoundland, a Rottweiler, and poodle dogs.

Hood also enjoys bird-watching and finds all aspects of nature precious. She demonstrates a passionate appreciation of the environment and a respect for all life.

Author Hood invites one and all to visit her websites at:

www.KarenJeanMatskoHood.com
www.KarenJeanMatskoHoodBlog.com
www.KarenJeanMatskoHoodBookstore.com
www.KarensKidsBooks.com

www.HoodFamilyBlog.com
www.HoodFamily.com

Author's Social Media

Friend her on **Facebook**: Karen Jean Matsko Hood Author Fan Page
Please Follow the Author on **Twitter**: @KarenJeanHood
Google Plus Profile: Karen Jean Matsko Hood
Pinterest.com/KarenJMHood

www.ingramcontent.com/pod-product-compliance
Lightning Source LLC
Chambersburg PA
CBHW060247100426
42742CB00011B/1673

Praise for Christmas Gifts-in-a-Jar
A Collection of Christmas Gifts-in-a-Jar Recipes
Gifts-in-a-Jar Cookbook Series – Book 1

…"We teach our children that gifts of time and homemade gifts are the best of all. Enjoy these **Christmas Gifts-in-a-Jar** recipes and make your own gifts."…

Dr. James G. Hood

…"Praise to **Christmas Gifts-in-a-Jar Cookbook** which has all the makings of a classic favorite. Now you too can prepare that dish that everyone wants the recipe for!

Author Karen Jean Matsko Hood presents a wide variety of Holiday treats.

Instead of the same routine, try something new and unexpected this year!"…

Ed Archambeault
Spokane, WA

Praise for Christmas Gifts-in-a-Jar
A Collection of Christmas Gifts-in-a-Jar Recipes
Gifts-in-a-Jar Cookbook Series – Book 1

…"**Christmas Gifts-in-a-Jar Cookbook** shows off the best of this holiday's offerings. You'll love the tone and feel of this cookbook that stands out from the rest."…

Allyson Schnabel
Editor, Teacher

…"You will enjoy making all the tantalizing dishes that inhabit the 320 pages of **Christmas Gifts-in-a-Jar Cookbook** that promises to be an added family tradition and a keepsake for many happy years to come."…

Mary Scripture
Graphic Designer